COLLABORATION

VISIONARIES SHARING A NEW WAY OF LIVING

Concept: Krystal Hille

Book Cover: Fyra

Editing: Vanessa Frazon Nelson

Formatting: Colleen Reagon Noon

Publishing: Hille House Publishing

CONTENTS

INTRODUCTION

We live in incredible times of transition. The old systems are fighting to survive, and new systems are emerging quietly and steadily. They are not fighting to overthrow the old, because they live outside of the duality of good or bad, right or wrong. They are simply creating a new timeline and new understanding of how to create advanced ways of living from a more aligned space.

Whilst mass-media feed us fear and propagate division in a desperate attempt to divide and conquer, there are new seedlings growing. Amongst the masses are bridge holders and light-code carriers who quietly and consciously hold the vibration and vision of the new world. It is already here, inside our hearts, at times buried beneath layers of fear, anxiety, and pain.

To step into collaboration, we must first release fear, scarcity, and the deeply ingrained belief that we must fight for our survival, fight for love, fight for recognition, fight for approval and belonging. The old matrix wants us to believe that life is a struggle, that we are not worthy to follow our inner guidance, instead look outside of ourselves for approval, so they can continue to exploit us.

The old system has fed us fears, so that our immune systems become weak, health problems skyrocket, and authentic connection based on emotional intelligence and unconditional love are few and far between. Misunderstandings occur, assumptions fly high, and judgement replaces compassionate understanding. All because collectively, we haven't yet fully tapped into self-love and self-respect, the cornerstones for effective collaboration and harmonious relationships.

With so much angst in the collective, how can we possibly collaborate?

When our first few levels of Maslov's hierarchy of needs are not met, self-actualisation is unattainable because we are preoccupied with the survival of the fittest. But there is hope. We can choose another way!

When we open our eyes to the possibility of infinite potential, when we begin to understand the laws of neuroplasticity and quantum physics, when we start to trust our inner knowing and visualise that which we innately know we came here to create, when we make it so real in our minds eye that we can touch it, taste it, feel it, when we surrender all else up to the divine over and over again, then we begin to disentangle from the matrix and set a movement in motion that creates the world we know we came here to build. It's an inside job. It starts with us.

The contributors of this book are the visionaries who have released the many layers of fear and dissolved most of their limiting ancestral and karmic programming of fighting for survival that results in competition and greed.

Scattered across the globe, they anchor higher vibrations onto this planet to hold steady that which is being birthed beyond the Piscean Age of competition, comparison, and the corruption of power, heralding in the Aquarian Age of collaboration, authentic connections, and heart-centred communities.

The intention of this book is to shine the spotlight on the collective shadow that is asking to be dissolved, and to provide inspiration, tools, and stories to release the remaining threads of our own hypocrisy, competition, and judgement so that we can embrace self-love, deep connection, and thus open the doors for true collaboration.

Spiritual Futurist Christof Melchizedek provides a powerful overview of the transition of the ages, the evolution of consciousness and how that leads us away from hierarchies towards decentralised, collaborative ways of being.

Next, Armida Martinez (Life & Mindset Coach), Cindy Cerecer (Principal of the International Colon Hydrotherapy Training Academy), Jayne Marquis (Homeopathic Doctor), and Jennifer Ackad (Embodiment and Transformation Coach), explore the idea of what it means to truly love and respect our innate self-worth and learn to truly collaborate with ourselves before entering into any other form of collaboration.

In the second section, Jaime Lund (Founder of Thrive Tribes Global), Jason Fisher, (bodyworker, therapist, and healer), Kelly Boucher (independent scholar, education consultant and personal breakthrough coach), as well as Vanessa Frazon Nelson (Publisher, Editor and Emotional Freedom Facilitator), take us deeper into what it means to collaborate in community, create a better future and think otherwise.

The third section is about collaboration in business. Adriana Monique Alvarez (USA Today Bestselling author and founder of AMA Publishing), Brigid Holder (USA Today Bestselling author and founder of the Art of Grace Publishing House), Claudia Spahr (international speaker and leadership mentor) and Sean Moloney (Founder of Digital Business Masters and the Blockchain Academy), take us from the cultivation of a collaborative business mindset, to introducing indigenous practices into modern business processes, to changing the way we think about money.

The final section of this book explores our collaboration with the Divine. A teacher of the Divine, Catherine Tetreault-Ayotte (Founder of the Sacred Path of The Priestess Retreats), Katerina Lenarcic (Quantum Light Master and Activator), and Olivia Grace (Transformational Law of Attraction Coach) share their stories of creating the ultimate collaboration with the unified field of infinite potential.

May their stories inspire and activate you into higher realms of consciousness.

May they ground you into deeper levels of self-love.

May they help you claim your unique place in this world; because when you do, collaboration becomes an effortless and expansive experience of deep connection and pure joy, from where you can manifest your best possible life.

May these pages reflect your highest essence back to you, and deepen the understanding of your unique story in the context of the collective journey of our human evolution, into a new era of awakened sovereignty and empowered collaboration.

With love,
Krystal Hille
Founder of Hille House Publishing

Part I

TRANSITIONING INTO THE CURRENCY OF COLLABORATION

CHRISTOF MELCHIZEDEK

THE EVOLUTION OF CONSCIOUSNESS, CRYPTO AND NEW WAYS OF COLLABORATION

Excerpt from the ***Conscious Crypto Manifesto*** by Christof Melchizedek

In this excerpt, I will share the big picture of the immense changes taking place in our world right now, the logical sequence of events unfolding, and how crypto is at the forefront of our evolution.

By the end, I hope you will sense what I do: That "Blockchain is Unity Consciousness expressing itself as technology."

We are currently experiencing a perfect storm of colliding technological trends creating an incredible opportunity for us individually and collectively. In this decade, we will witness unprecedented technological breakthroughs, and as a result, massive societal reorganization.

Having the foresight and comprehension of these sweeping upgrades will not only position you for profits but will also catapult you into a new financial reality.

The changes coming to society will be fast and immense; if you do not keep up with them, you will be left behind. The beauty of foresight is that you can position yourself to take advantage of The Great Wealth Transfer, as money drains from the old legacy system into a new one now being created.

THE CONSCIOUS CRYPTO TRUE MACRO POSITION STATEMENT

We are on the precipice of a tremendous systemic shift that will take us from centralized hierarchy and control to decentralized systems of organization and transfer of value. This change emerges from the morphogenetic field of higher consciousness. Blockchain and distributed ledger is unity consciousness expressing itself as technology and will formulate the organizing system of every primary system holding society together for the next several hundred years.

I believe this change is inevitable. As human consciousness and this technology continue to expand alongside each other, we will eventually arrive at the promised land of a much more open, free, decentralized, harmonious, abundant society.

THE ENERGETIC THEME OF THE AQUARIAN AGE

There is overwhelming scientific evidence that at the most fundamental level, everything is energy. The old model of reality, in which the solar system consisted of electrons and protons as tiny, solid, planet-like structures whizzing around a larger interior neutron in an atom, has been completely debunked.

The reality is that everything is energy, and energy is everything. Energy consists of sound, vibration, and light. These are the primal forces affecting the collective on Earth.

Furthermore, energy is not static; it moves and evolves and has information stored in it that we humans pick up and are affected by. These energetic archetypes are supported in the celestial spheres and held together astrologically to create the energy fields that we respond to.

These astrological archetype templates are constantly moving through cycles that affect us.

We are energetic, conscious beings, and our luminous bio-field is always energetically receiving information from the Unified Field. When that information changes, we respond differently.

The basic principle of astrology is *"as above, so below,"* which means that the planets in our solar system hold energetic archetypes and transmit these to our planet, which our bio-energy field and DNA templates pick up as information.

The human body is a holographic projection of sound, vibration, and light built upon a holographic template of consciousness, easily affected by astrological influences.

Even the late American financier and banker, J.P. Morgan, knew that the energy of the Universe affects wealth, which is why he is famous for saying, "Millionaires don't use astrology, billionaires do."

Each planet has a unique influence on the Earth that contributes to what Rupert Sheldrake, the British biologist, termed the morphogenetic field.

Humanity's collective consciousness mirrors the astrological influences of the time-space epoch we now find ourselves navigating.

Thus, astrological forces send light and information into humanity's morphogenetic field, creating a subtle yet powerful organizing current.

This is *True Macro.*

To fully comprehend the global societal changes we are going through, we'll need to examine the archetypal influences of the outgoing Piscean Age with the incoming Aquarian Age.

Every 200 or so years, our planet is in a particular astrological energetic template. From 0 A.D. to the present, we have been in the Age of Pisces.

For the next 2000 years, we will be in the Aquarian Age.

The primary difference between the Piscean Age we are migrating out of and the Aquarian Age we are entering is that the Piscean Age had a vertical hierarchy, while the Aquarian Age will be organized in a horizontal network, opening the world up to true equality.

THE PISCEAN AGE CENTRAL TENET

The primary tenet of people navigating through the Piscean Age has been, "I Believe". and they have directed their lives from this lens. They found structures, gurus, religions, ideologies, sects, companies, and charismatic leaders to guide their beliefs. A few people held knowledge they passed down as ideologies, commandments, dogma, philosophy, or governmental dictates.

The masses did not need to know the secrets of life directly but only needed to follow someone else who did. People would latch onto the concepts from a leader and formulate a core belief based upon a philosophy. From a particular set of beliefs, they would develop their behaviors, which then framed their life.

A natural consequence of this energetic relationship in the Piscean Age was that formulating beliefs through intermediaries created vertical power structures of top-down influence.

The gradual consolidation of information and power over the past 2000 years means today we have one interconnected super-entity.

This super-entity is an elite group of powerful corporations that control three core arenas of society: media, military, and money. This small group of affiliated organizations has its influences across hundreds of thousands of corporations so that only 23 companies currently control and manipulate assets valued at more than $183 trillion.

The natural end has arrived for the Piscean "I Believe" consciousness.

THE AQUARIAN AGE CENTRAL TENET

The primary tenet of the Aquarian Age is, 'I Know,' which marks a fundamental shift in how we now access information directly, with no need for intermediaries.

This changes everything.

Consciousness is now available to all because the quantum field vibrations are finer and faster, which means more and more of us are guided by our direct connection to the Source of all things.

Therefore, we will eventually move away from the vertical, centralized super-entity with access to all the information and control, as we saw in the Piscean Age, to an interconnected, horizontal network of seamlessly transferring decentralized information.

We are now in the Information Age, where nothing is secret anymore. Everything is available instantly to everyone, everywhere, which will create much greater equality over the long term.

Our focus is no longer on securing a personal identity as given to us by an external authority, but instead on knowing ourselves as already whole and complete. We are the leaders of ourselves.

We inherently trust the direct access we have to Source consciousness. In this age, humanity will rely less and less on external sources for their information and what they need to believe because deep down, everyone will *know*.

We already see this playing out with the public's growing distrust of government policies and practices and the media's partisan views. Those who are evolving and expanding their consciousness have already switched off their mainstream news sources, responsible for shaping misperceptions for the last several decades.

The technological infrastructure that will hold and host our attention and consciousness in a horizontal network is already being built. This will allow for a seamless transfer of information and data in a permissionless, decentralized, transparent, censorship-resistant, and programmable form.

That technology is blockchain, the technology of the Aquarian Age.

This energetic shift will bring radical changes to our lives as the top-down, centralized control structures give way to horizontal, decentralized networks by the people, and people.

THE TRANSITION OF THE AGES

Since we are talking about a 2000-year cycle, there is no key transition date from one age to another. The frequency and energy have a period where they overlap, phasing in and out of reality. This means there is a point where a blend and a bifurcation take place.

Some people are still accessing and operating on the energy of the old age. They continue to build and add to their central hierarchical systems to consolidate power. Blissfully unaware that there is a new way emerging, their consciousness simply hasn't opened up to the higher frequency because they are so heavily invested in the rewards of their efforts under the old ways of doing things.

However, others are tapping into this new frequency. They are having their consciousness inspired by fresh ideas, new ways of seeing the world, and better comprehension of how to organize ourselves for sovereignty, freedom, transparency, and open access to information.

These are the visionaries dreaming of the world to be a better place and using their skills and talents to be part of this sweeping global financial, political, and cultural revolution that has open access for all.

Humanity is at a cross road and two realities will be coexisting for some time. It's a bifurcation, a point or area at which something divides into two branches or parts.

We see this now in the formulation of the new blockchain technology that is disrupting the legacy financial system, thereby making banks redundant. With this new technology, you own your assets directly, without intermediaries. You are the bank.

In the financial world, we currently have two systems existing simultaneously. The old system was established and set up under the influence of the previous energetic template of the Piscean Age. This is a system of structure involving intermediaries, such as banks holding your money on your behalf and brokers taking fat commissions for exchanging value between parties.

Then we have the new system being built now as we enter the Aquarian Age. We now have options, such as bitcoin, that allow you to hold your own money directly without intermediaries for genuine peer-to-peer transactions. Another product, called Ethereum, allows for trusted exchange of value between parties without intermediaries, based on certain conditions being met. These are known as Smart Contracts.

We are simultaneously watching the birth of the new system and the death of the old system, and we can participate in the massive transfer of value and assets that will take place over the next decade as the legacy system crumbles and the new system rises.

FURTHER ASTROLOGICAL INFLUENCES

We have recently moved through something known as the Great Conjunction. A conjunction is where two or more planets are at almost the same position in the horoscope. Their energies and influences unite, creating an amplified and powerful force.

The Great Conjunction is when the two biggest planets, Saturn and Jupiter, merge their fields of influence. This event is considered one of the most powerful, catalyzing energetic forces in Astrology and is usually followed by dramatic societal change.

Saturn represents rules, boundaries, structures, and systems, which we can see dismantling and crumbling, now that era has passed. Jupiter is here to support the rebuilding of a New Earth, with innovative ways of living, working, trading, and operating in the world.

This particular alignment at zero degrees of Aquarius is important because this is the zeroing in of the Aquarian Age.

The Earth element influences have ruled our planet for 800 years, which is all about building and constructing physical things, such as our modern cities and societies.

With the great conjunction, we say goodbye to those heavy influences and welcome in a new ruler, the element of air, for the next 800 years.

As we leave the more dense earth energy, our transition will be towards more intellectual, inventive, faster-moving air energy.

I see the Aquarian themes of humanitarianism and technology merging, so technology can be the vehicle that takes us from centralized control to decentralized freedom. With new advancements being made every day in blockchain technology, we are living at the threshold of what's being called **The Second Renaissance.**

Traditionally, third world countries have been excluded from the banking system, creating 2.5 billion unbanked people globally who don't have access to financial services.

With the advent of smartphones, the internet, and the growing crypto-sphere movement, we now have the power and the potential to liberate the unbanked into financial sovereignty through the power of technology.

Imagine the creative expansion possible when the unbanked population suddenly has access to financial resources and instruments. Rather than handouts, which do nothing to empower communities, hand-ups can bring people into economic sovereignty. This is the highest level of support that would truly benefit these communities.

This is why I am so excited about the power of this technology; it is a revolution that can change the world by circumventing the middlemen and vertical columns of power in every single industry.

This technology is the supporting infrastructure that can be the scaffolding to build the energetic frequency coming onto the planet right now. Remember, networks are the hallmark of the Aquarian Age, which we are transitioning into.

The crypto-sphere and the global trend of decentralization are the physical building blocks of a whole new way of transacting value and sharing resources, potentially disrupting every central agency in the world.

Finally, we have the technology to disperse resources into the hands of the people, giving the power back to where it belongs.

To the people.

People are now clearly seeing the imbalances and grievances created by centralized control structures while witnessing the deterioration of their living standards, purchasing power, and sovereignty.

It is only a matter of time before the themes of decentralization become a core belief held in the morphogenetic field of the collective. When enough people hold a core belief, it acts as an 'on' switch for the collective, and we then have mass adoption.

A collective core belief in the benefits of decentralization will catalyze a seismic transfer of trust from the old centralized systems into the new crypto-sphere ecosystem. At some point, the mass consciousness of The People will demand a new way of operating that solves the systemic agency problem. They will request more open and transparent ways of functioning through every level of society.

We are now birthing the technology that can solve these issues inherent in a centralized society. This new technology is emerging from the natural evolution of humanity, though it has accelerated over the last 40 years.

This acceleration is part of the Great Digital Disruption.

THE FOUR PHASES OF THE DIGITAL DISRUPTION

Change is something that some people welcome, and others try to avoid. Either way, change is not only inevitable, it's also natural and necessary.

Another word for change is evolution.

Change itself has an evolution; it goes from detectable to clear to accepted before finally becoming the new normal.

Individuals and industries might know about the change in the detectable stage, but its impact hasn't been recognized yet. As with any change, this stage challenges us to reexamine our own story and open ourselves up to a growth mindset. Alternatively, we can choose to maintain willful ignorance.

In the clear phase, change takes hold, and new initiatives are developed to support the incoming adjustments. Pitfalls of poorly navigating this stage include reluctance, unwillingness, or nearsightedness.

The accepted phase of change, also called 'the inevitable'—requires a shift of resources and a team of supporters. Power struggles and fear are the limiting factors that prevent a smooth transition from the old to the inevitable.

We are currently in the CLEAR phase of transition, as people are aware of this new technology that is slowly becoming our new normal. This progress is part of our path and our destiny. Even in the higher levels of centralized power, it's accepted as inevitable.

Since it is inevitable, centralized corporations and governments are adjusting their playbooks to introduce this technology to their customers and constituents by setting up the legal framework and onboarding ramps to bring people into *their* version of this world.

As you shall see, each phase of the digital disruption stands on the shoulders of the last. The blockchain breakthrough would not be possible without the other stages that preceded it.

PHASE ONE: 1980'S THE PERSONAL COMPUTER

Starting in the 1980's computer science began emerging into smaller and smaller units of processing power until such a time as the computer hard drive could fit onto someone's desk. Before this, servers and processors needed large wardrobe-sized spaces to host all the hard drives and processors required to perform functions.

Moore's law observes that the number of transistors in a dense integrated circuit (IC) doubles about every two years. This has been true in the technology space for almost 40 years. As the large computer processors became smaller and smaller, we finally had one that could fit our desk, and the personal computer was born. As they became even smaller and more affordable, they replaced or disrupted typewriters and facsimiles until almost everyone in the western world had access to a PC.

PHASE TWO: THE INTERNET

Before the internet, these computers functioned in isolation; there was no swapping of data or information. Each PC operated as a silo of information, and very few computers were networked together or leveraging their resources.

The internet came along and changed all that. Like today with blockchain, the first modems were slow, and the internet had few use cases.

As the processing power improved and internet connection speeds increased, we slowly layered in the applications we see today. The internet was built on a protocol (foundation layer) known as HTTP, which stands for Hypertext Transfer Protocol. It paved the way for a standard operating language that would allow all internet sites to communicate and talk to one another.

It is the protocol upon which the modern internet was built; however, it was designed to transfer information only. It was never designed, at the protocol layer, for security or any transfer of value.

Hence, today we have issues with internet security and privacy, and you cannot transfer anything of digital value without being copied and sent around the internet.

For example, if you download an ebook, nothing stops you from transferring it to your contact list in 30 seconds. There was no digital scarcity, or security built into the HTTP protocol, simply because it wasn't thought of at the time.

No one knew the internet would become the central operating system of the planet 30-40 years later. As speed and interconnectedness improved, applications were built on the protocol layer, and the great race to create value on the internet began.

Established, big-name companies such as Kodak and Blockbuster became obsolete overnight, as new technology came on board. These innovators, not concerned with protecting old interests, found ways to disrupt the existing dominant companies who'd captured most of the value in the days before the second digital disruption.

Over time this 'value capture' has consolidated into the hands of a few mega-corporations who have built business models based on information by developing networks and monetizing these networks in the second and third phases of the digital disruption.

These companies and their stocks are known as FAANG, comprised of:

Facebook

Amazon

Apple

Netflix

Google

Facebook and Google created and widely distributed free products knowing they could monetize their growing network by serving up ads to their customers.

There is a saying in technology, "If the product is free to use, you are the product." By capturing people's most valued digital asset, their personal data, the megalithic corporations who built applications on the old protocols are serving us up ads based upon our browsing history, subscriptions, and online preferences.

Even Google algorithms adjust website options based upon your browsing history data. These massive corporations have become all-powerful, influenced by political agendas, and offer search engine results based upon preferences of the political regime they support.

This has led to massive internet censorship, as these large tech giants shadow or physically ban content providers who do not align with their political interests. Internet censorship, according to political ideals in another time, was called propaganda. Propaganda is simply communication used to influence an audience to further an agenda.

PHASE THREE: SMARTPHONES

The third phase of the digital revolution has been smartphones. Smartphones have put the power of the internet into the hands of potentially everyone. The influence of this cannot be overstated because now we can unlock global opportunities for all beings - including those living in third-world countries.

With the Star Link network (https://www.starlink.com) coming online fully, we will have high-speed global internet coverage. With high-speed internet coverage and smartphone devices, we will be able to get opportunities into the hands of the 2.5 billion unbanked people and bring them into a new financial landscape now emerging with the advent of the fourth digital disruption.

PHASE FOUR: BLOCKCHAIN TECHNOLOGY

We stand at the precipice of the greatest disrupter of all the phases. This is a bold statement given how dramatically different our daily lives look now because of personal computers, the internet, and smartphone devices.

But none of these have created the fundamental sociological impact on the fabric of society that blockchain will make. Blockchain is heralding a whole new way of organizing ourselves. It is a new ideology moving us from "we are ruled" to "we rule ourselves."

It is moving us from Hierarchy to Synarchy. Synarchy refers to joint or shared leadership, where it's no longer a top-down directive requiring the majority to follow the will of a few. But instead, synarchy is a collective self-organizational movement, where people act from inspiration rather than coercion.

THE DECENTRALIZED INEVITABILITY

Blockchain technology will create a seismic shift in the whole way society organizes itself. It is the beginning of the era of decentralized networks. Over a more extended period, such as 50 years, the proliferation of decentralized networks that run the systems of society will seem normal.

Until recently, the majority of society's networks have been centralized. Today the digital disruption of blockchain technology is creating the ability to run decentralized and distributed forms of organization.

This means everything can be organized peer to peer or on a user-to-user basis. This is possible because each user has a complete copy of the database. We no longer need a central authorizer to know what's happened on the network.

When each user has a complete copy of the database and gets independently verified by its users, you have a self-regulating transparency, truth, and authenticity system. This is the big change coming to society, and this concept will be built into every area of society in the years ahead.

Blockchain is the technology that will deliver decentralization on a global scale. It can disrupt all the middlemen and middle service layers that have traditionally taken fat fees and commissions for services.

This change is inevitable as we move from a structure that is misaligned at its core to a fully aligned energetic system that will host the world's commerce in the future.

With negative interest rates, hyperinflation, deficit spending, corruption, financial nepotism, and double-speak, the current economic system is crumbling, and something better is being built to replace it. Change is coming.

The preparation for Humanity's evolution from a fixed, controlled, centralized economy to a decentralized, digital world economy has been occurring for many decades as we have been moving through the phases of the Four Digital Disruptions.

Each of these technological milestones brought us closer to unification and collaboration where anyone can directly communicate and do business with anyone else. We are currently in a transition between the birthing of a new paradigm in technology and mainstream adoption. This is the point of maximum opportunity for early investors and adopters.

We are on the precipice of an incredible quantum leap and expansion in adoption. The large institutions who made it big in the legacy financial system have seen the writing on the walls.

Those who have the vision can see what is coming and are willing to learn about the Crypto-Sphere (the ecosystem built as the network of this new system) and will be the recipient of the Greatest Wealth Transfer in human history.

Blockchain technology and cryptocurrencies are creating a new financial industry of freedom and sovereign choice at their core. These advancements will change how we relate to others (no middle man); it will ensure privacy (tamper-proof), enhance communication (fewer limitations), and allow for greater self-expression as you choose how to live your abundant, economic life.

This industry is also about innovation and automation. We'll see more advancement in monetary policies in the crypto space in the next 10-years than we've seen in the last 100-years.

There will also be more innovations in financial engineering as the construction of financial projects and the marketplaces that trade them expand. There will also be more movement of wealth as money travels on crypto rails 24/7.

Bitcoin and most other crypto protocols are decentralized, meaning no one person or company controls or oversees the network. All previous digital coin attempts (and there were several) required a central authority that was able to confirm transactions.

The need for a central confirming authority was their downfall because the government was able to shut down each and every one of them. When you are decentralized—there is no one to "shut down"—you would have to shut down the internet to stop Bitcoin.

The main reason for requiring a central authority in the past was no one could solve the "double-spend" problem. The *double-spend* problem arises when a malicious person attempts to spend their digital coins simultaneously with two or more recipients.

Without a central authority standing in the middle of all transactions, each "spend" appears to be valid to all recipients receiving the digital coins. Initially, when checked, the malicious person does have the balance in their account for each recipient.

This is easily stopped in the old centralized system because each transaction has to pass through a central authority that keeps track of everyone's balance. This is how all financial transactions happen today in the fiat world, fiat money being the term used to describe government issued currency that is not backed by a physical commodity, such as gold or silver.

However, Satoshi Nakamoto (the name used by the presumed pseudonymous person or persons who developed Bitcoin) was able to use technology to accomplish this same protection against the *double-spend*. The Bitcoin network has thousands of copies of a single database (think of a ledger of transactions). They all agree on each and every transaction, down to the satoshi (the smallest unit of a Bitcoin, and there are 100 million of them in each Bitcoin).

Therefore, *double-spends* cannot happen. The malicious actor can attempt a *double-spend,* but within two or three confirmations (confirmations are blocks of transactions added to the blockchain), one of the transactions will be permanently recorded into the blockchain. All the others will be thrown out as invalid transactions.

Only valid transactions that have the necessary balance can exist on the blockchain. This is why recipients of bitcoins must wait up to a half-hour for three confirmations to be completed before considering a Bitcoin transfer to be final and irreversible.

When you consider that cryptocurrency transactions only take half an hour to send (anywhere in the world) and finalize, this is much better than what people deal with today with electronic fiat transfers.

Credit card transactions are not resolved for days, and chargebacks (essentially refunds for the customer), can happen up to 90 days after the transactions are completed. Checks take up to a week to process and can be stopped or be fraudulent. Bitcoin transactions are complete and permanent after just a 1/2 hour. No reversal is possible.

Another breakthrough technology was that for the first time, something digital could be unique and not copyable. If you are given anything digital (before Bitcoin), you could make thousands of copies of it. With Bitcoin, each coin is unique and cannot be copied.

One Bitcoin is one Bitcoin; it cannot be copied. You can send this one Bitcoin directly to anyone in the world with a Bitcoin wallet with no intermediate involved. Today, this same technology is being used to power all Non-Fungible Tokens (NFT), capturing the headlines these days.

Bitcoin is a borderless, permissionless, and uncensorable digital store of value. And with the advent of the Lightning Network, it is starting to be a true currency that can be used for daily purchases.

For example, all of El Salvador is currently using Bitcoin on the Lightning Network, which allows many, many, thousands of transactions per second for a fraction of a penny in transaction fees.

El Salvador is just the beginning. We expect many other sovereign nation states to follow suit and give their people the opportunity to participate in the world's first Hard Money. Their purchasing power will be protected by an appreciating asset rather than the depreciating fiat money so many countries still use today.

Having Bitcoin as a national currency means that suddenly El Salvador and other countries will gain sovereignty over the USD hegemony that currently exists while giving their citizens the ability to participate in the Global Digital Economy.

WHAT ARE THE KEY FEATURES OF BLOCKCHAIN TECHNOLOGY

- permissionless
- decentralized
- trustless
- transparent
- censorship-resistant
- programmable

WHY YOU MIGHT WANT TO PAY ATTENTION TO WHAT IS HAPPENING

Since we are still early in this big transition from the centralized world to the decentralized world, there is an incredible opportunity to capture value as the build-out of the crypto-sphere continues.

Investing in the correct protocols and applications today can create generational wealth as the value begins to drain out of the legacy system into this new one.

The crypto-sphere and blockchain technology is the foundation of the Internet of Value. It is the foundation upon which the high-tech world of the future is being built and constructed. This transfer from the old analog systems to the new high-tech digital systems is still in its infancy.

By paying attention to this space now, you can massively amplify and increase your purchasing power as the money from the legacy system drains into this system. We are witnessing the greatest Wealth Transfer in human history, and you can participate in it and change your financial trajectory.

As deeply aware beings living in the Age of Aquarius, we are all being called onto a path of accelerated spiritual evolution. We can manifest prosperity for all by investing in value-aligned cryptocurrencies and blockchain projects, which will be the systems and infrastructure transitioning us into a higher frequency reality.

We are the architects of a more evolved vision and reality. We can choose self-empowerment, sovereignty, and financial freedom.

We can use this technology to free and liberate ourselves, our community, and the world.

I love you,
Christof

ABOUT THE AUTHOR

CHRISTOF MELCHIZEDEK

Christof Melchizedek delivers insights that are relevant and inspiring. He's an entrepreneur, speaker, shamanic facilitator, and highly sought-after leadership coach. He is also a father, a husband, and a man who believes that creating a conscious community of change begins in our own hearts and homes.

Christof has more than 25 years of experience working with Fortune 500 executives, pro-athletes and entrepreneurs, and experts in health, performance, the healing arts, psychology, and leadership. Coined a 'spiritual futurist,' Christof's gift for integrating higher spiritual concepts with physical, real-world macro trends gives his audiences holistic, practical tools to implement immediately.

As the founder of an underground Financial Liberation movement called the Conscious Crypto Circle, Christof is helping spiritually evolved people get positioned for the Great Wealth Transfer through the paradigm-shifting world of crypto-currencies, assets, and projects.

He is passionate about supporting soul-centered entrepreneurs, leaders, and change-makers by providing the framework, skill sets, and energetic intelligence necessary to help them grow personally and professionally to change the world.

Whether on the live or virtual stage, Christof is a dynamic speaker with a powerful presence who captures the hearts and minds of his audience. As a frequent guest on some of the most popular podcasts and shows in his field, Christof is deeply valued for his insights, predictions, and passion for redefining leadership in these evolving times.

Christof's personal website: www.christof.love
Christof's conscious crypto education network: https://www.consciouscryptocircle.com

Part II

COLLABORATION WITH SELF

ARMIDA ABREU MARTINEZ

A LOVE FOR ONENESS!

I clearly remember the day that I had my first "I can't do this anymore" from a place of authenticity and surrender. It was a rainy and cool morning in the spring of 2019, I had just returned home from dropping off the kids at school. On this particular day I had woken up feeling defeated, anxious, stuck, guilty, and ashamed which quite honestly was not any different than any other day, however, on this day there was a sense of surrendering and letting go of my energy that I had never felt before.

I remember walking into my home office and just feeling heavy and supported all at the same time. I looked around my office and out the window and into the clouds up above and I just sat there completely motionless for about 10 minutes just staring into the sky and the clouds. I somehow felt peace in my heart and in my soul, and for the first time, in a weird and unexplainable way, I felt supported and like everything was going to be okay. At that moment I dropped down on my knees and just cried. I cried and I cried, and I screamed and I screamed for a good 20 minutes, and then I did something I had never done before. I asked the universe for guidance and for help. At that moment I stopped blaming everyone else for my misfortunes and took responsibility for my life. I decided to be open and available to the solutions to my problems and to start acting from a place of love and compassion not only for myself but for others. I stood up, I looked at my vision board (which had been hanging on my wall for about 2 years now) and I made the decision to commit to myself and to my dreams fully and without any resistance.

I could feel the dampness on my shirt from all of the tears that had streamed down my face and onto the chest area of my shirt almost as though they were being accumulated in my heart area to be absorbed and transmuted into unconditional love. I don't think I had ever cried that hard in my life.

I took a couple of deep breaths, and I asked clearly to the universe for what I authentically wanted from my heart and I expressed gratitude in advance for the love and support that I somehow knew that I was going to get. I am not exactly sure how I felt so sure about this, but I somehow did. I felt this deep connection at that moment not only to myself, but the world around me which was something I had never felt before. I knew at that very moment that I was going to be okay and that things were going to work out for me.

I then walked into my gray-colored bathroom, which somehow matched the color of the skies, and I bravely looked at myself in the mirror. My eyes were red and swollen from all of the crying, but somehow through the pain I was able to see a spark in my eyes that I had never seen before. At that very moment, I felt whole, complete, alive, and, most importantly, loved and accepted, a feeling that I had never felt before. It was the most beautiful feeling in the world. I felt like I was finally home.

But, if I am just coming home, where have I been all of this time? Why did I leave in the first place? And most importantly, how do I stay here forever? Because, you see, even though I had experienced this just for a few short minutes in linear human time, it felt very familiar and like an eternity to my heart and my soul. It was as though I had just woken up from a nightmare and into this new and empowering reality, a reality where fear, judgement, anger, guilt, and shame were all an illusion. An illusion that was keeping me feeling resentful, stuck, powerless and closed off to unconditional love for others, for my environment and most importantly for myself. And this, my friend, is the day that led me down the path to my radical spiritual awakening. A path that has led me to be in complete collaboration with myself, with the universe, and with others.

I think now it's a good time to get into the juiciness of how it all started and what led to this illusion of lack and separation in the first place. First of all, let me just say that there were many things, people and experiences that led me down this perceived lonely and lost path for a very long time.

It all started when (drum roll please) when I was a kid. I know, right. What a shocker, as if you are completely surprised to hear this. And no, I am not being sarcastic, it's just that I am now completely aware that at some level we all experience some form of childhood trauma that if not processed successfully can negatively affect how we perceive our world as adults. And when that happens we grow up to see the world from a limited perspective through the lens of fear, lack and separation, which we somehow subconsciously believe are normal and for our benefit because those feelings bring us a sense of safety, security and control.

Okay, I know, I know I've gone off on a tangent and I haven't jumped into my story. So here it is:

I was the beautiful product of two beautiful and unhealed people that genuinely loved each other and had their best interest for themselves and for me at heart. But when I was 3, they separated and I went to live with my maternal grandmother. My maternal grandmother was truly amazing and I was very lucky to have had her in my life. Still, it was not enough for me. I wanted to be with my parents. I felt abandoned by them and that led me to believe at a very young age that I wasn't good enough to be loved.

My mom was in and out of my life for a few years. She would go away for months (or years) at a time and I wouldn't see her at all.

My dad was nowhere to be found (not completely his fault though); my parents separated in not the most loving way and they had zero contact with one another. There were times that my dad would come from the States to visit his family in this new country that I now resided in. (Oh yeah, I forgot to mention earlier that when my parents separated my mother moved back to her native country, the beautiful island of the Dominican Republic.) So I was separated from my father not only by Mom but also by the distance of living in two different worlds.

I still remember on certain occasions when my dad was visiting his native land, he would make his way to try to see me, only to find an empty home because if my mom happened to be around she would turn off the lights and make me hide. It's so crazy to see how she was never around for me but she somehow knew when my dad was around and would magically appear in my life to hide me from him. It's like she had superpowers. So as a child, I had a physically, and emotionally unavailable mom, as well as a physically unavailable dad, although not entirely his fault, and I can confidently say now that it wasn't my mother's fault either. It took me many years to realize this.

Anyways, I don't want to go off on a tangent again, so back to my story: When I was 8 years old, my grandmother had sent me to visit my dad for the summer. I was excited to finally meet my dad and get to know him. I was also excited to be going back to the country that I was born in, and to experience what life was like in the States. You see, I was born in Brooklyn, NY 8 years prior but had only lived there until I was 3 years old. I had no clear memory of what it was like to live there.

I forgot to mention one of the most important things about coming to the States and meeting my dad. I was also going to be spending time with my brother, who was my flesh and blood from both my dad and my mom. He was a year younger than me and when our parents separated he went to live with my Paternal grandmother. She often traveled from the States to the Dominican Republic and when she was in the Dominican Republic she would make an effort to pick me up and spend time with me, which was great because I was able to spend time with my brother as well.

Spending time with my brother was the best, especially when we weren't fighting with each other. We were both very passionate and active kids so we would get into trouble often. Especially my brother, he was always curious and unafraid to try things out even if it meant that he could get into trouble, which he did quite often. He was also an instigator and loved to push my buttons, which I must say were very easy to push. I could easily go from 0 to 100 with just the slightest touch. Must have been my fiery temper from being both a natural redhead and an Aries... I know—talk about a powerful combination. I still don't know how I managed to survive my childhood without any broken bones or serious injuries. I'm sure my guardian angels didn't know what they were signing up for when they made the decision to guard me. So I think that this is an appropriate time to thank them for all of their hard work and commitment to my safety.

Anyways, back to my story. I am sure that by now, you have noticed that I have a little bit of ADD, but I assure you that I only get it only when I am extremely excited. I mean, how can I not be? I am sitting at home at my desk with a lit candle, a gratitude rock that has the word 'love' engraved on it next to me, and I am reliving my life from a totally different perspective. How amazing and empowering is that? And, that is my wish and hope for you. So, if you have ever felt alone, abandoned and unloved, I assure you that you are not alone. So please, keep reading, it does get better, I promise.

Now back to when I was 8 years old and coming to the States to spend the summer with my dad, my brother, and I forgot to mention earlier, my beautiful half-sister and, like, if that wasn't enough, my stepmom. Yes, my dad had remarried. His new wife was a lot younger than him and very beautiful. She had curly, dirty-blonde hair, pretty, dark brown eyes and nice full lips. Oh, and she was also very pregnant with my new baby sister.

That summer was one of the best summers of my life. My dad worked a lot and my stepmother took care of us during that time. I can't even imagine how it must have been for her to be pregnant and caring for 3 very active kids between the ages of 7 and 9. We lived in an apartment building across the street from a big park that had a huge playground. We would wake up early and go there to play almost every day. On the weekends my dad would bring us to the beach with a big group of other family members. I didn't realize how big my family was and how fun they were.

They loved to party and music and dancing were a must in our reunions no matter where they were. I loved the fact that my dad and I shared such a special connection to music. Music can be so healing, especially when you feel lonely. That summer my dad took us to visit the Statue of Liberty, Times Square, 42nd Street and Rockefeller Center in New York City. I had the best time of my life that summer. I can still remember it like it was yesterday. I am so grateful for that experience.

When the end of the summer came my brother went back to live with our paternal grandmother, my sister went back home to live with her mother in Puerto Rico, and I decided to stay and live with my dad, his new wife and my soon-to-be-born baby sister. I was excited to live with my dad, to finally have the love and affection from one of my parents, to start a new school, make new friends and live my best 8-year-old life.

I quickly realized that my 8-year-old life was not going to be as perfect as I thought. My dad was not the most emotionally available person, so let's just say that even though he was present physically, he was not present emotionally at all. My stepmother, bless her soul, did the best that she could to take care of me and to show me love, but I think I was closed off to it and I never really gave her a fair chance because I was afraid to get hurt, at an unconscious level, that is, or maybe I just didn't now how to receive and accept love. I can't complain much about living with them. I had all of my physical needs taken care of but I still felt a hole in my heart and a disconnection to everyone around me including my dad and my stepmom. My little sister was my only real connection because, well, she didn't talk and I gave her a lot of attention so she loved being around me, and that made me feel loved and accepted. So to say that she was a blessing in my life is understatement.

When I was 16 years old we moved from NY to Massachusetts to a city called Worcester. My dad and stepmom were tired of living paycheck to paycheck in NY and they wanted to start new somewhere else, and in a place with the potential for growth and expansion. I was not happy to leave NY. I had a lot of great childhood friendships that I did not want to leave behind. I was also almost done with 10th grade and I had just 2 more years of high school to complete but I had no choice as I could not provide for myself at that time. So here I was In a new state, a new city and a new school.

I just realized that I forgot to mention earlier that my brother was living with us. My brother came to live with us about 2 to 3 years after I had decided to stay.

Anyways, life in Worcester wasn't too bad, we all adjusted to this new environment rather quickly.

When I was 17, my dad and my stepmother started to have relationship issues and my brother and I felt that a lot of it was because of us, or to be more specific, him. My brother was quite a rebel and he was always getting into trouble, which was causing a lot of stress to my dad's and stepmom's relationship. So he decided to leave and go live with a friend and I left with him. I wasn't going to let my brother be out there alone. We were going to do this together because we were the only ones to understand each other and the pain that we felt, although we never actually tried to tell anyone else about it.

Living with a friend only lasted a few short months as my paternal grandmother moved back to the States to live with us. I am so grateful for that woman. She has sacrificed so much for her family. She embodies strength, confidence, wisdom and courage. Living with my grandmother and my brother was fun and exciting, and a happy new experience.

I lived with my grandmother until I was 20 years old and made the decision to move in with my boyfriend, whom I had been dating for almost a year and his amazing family. I have great memories about them and how I was treated. They always made me feel like part of the family. They were, and still are some of the most amazing people I know, and I am truly grateful for them and for the experience that I had with them. When my boyfriend and I broke up, I think I was more sad about losing his family than I was about losing him. I mean he was, and still is a great guy but we were young and grew apart. Our separation was not traumatic, as we were both on the same page. I was 21 years old when this happened and I didn't want to move back home, so I moved in with my best friend and her family for almost a year. I had a great experience with them as well. They were, and still are a very united and loving family and I felt loved and accepted there. Shortly after my breakup I started to date this guy I had known for a long time. Things between us moved rather quickly. Within just a few months we were engaged, and then just a few short months after that we were married.

My first year of marriage was fun and difficult at the same time. There was a part of me that felt proud and excited about this new 'wife' role, but there was also a part of me that felt scared and worried. Did I make the right decision? Did I marry the right guy?

Am I going to be a good wife? Do I want kids? If so, when and how many? I was really getting over my head and I was putting a lot of pressure on myself. To top it off, 'Ms. Independent' me had to now take someone else's feelings into consideration when making decisions because any decision I made was now going to affect not just me, but him as well since we were together in this partnership. I'm sure things for him weren't that easy either, as he had some adjustments to do himself. However, we survived that first year, with some tears, fears and a whole lot of arguments.

One of our earlier arguments in life somehow ended with me literally ripping my tank-top open with my bare hands. Not one of my proudest moments, for sure, but it was a great thing that he had a good sense of humor. There I was in front of him with my tank top completely ripped apart and with my breast exposed, feeling shameful and scared, and all he could do is give me a strange look and say, 'I am not sure if I should be scared or turned on right now', which lightened up the mood and left us both laughing at the situation.

We had many fun times and arguments along the way but we somehow found a way to make it work. After being married for almost 7 years, we decided it was time to grow our family and have a baby. I got off the birth control pills and 2 months later I was pregnant with my first child. My beautiful baby girl was born In December of 2009. I was extremely happy and grateful to be a mom. It was something that I have always known I wanted to be. When my first born was 2 years old, we decided that we were ready for baby #2, and a year later we welcomed our second daughter. Life was very busy. I was a full time employee at a non-profit social work agency, raising 2 little girls. My husband had made the decision to start a business to better provide for us but this new responsibility took him away from the family a lot. I felt like I was a single parent and I felt very lonely and unsupported.

Have you ever felt alone even though you were surrounded by people? That's how I felt in my own home. My husband and I were so disconnected that I was planning to walk away from my marriage. But before I had a chance to pull the plug, I found out that I was pregnant with my 3rd child. I had never had an abortion before but, I had considered it. I couldn't go through with it, so I made the choice to stay in the relationship and keep the pregnancy.

During my pregnancy I developed postpartum depression. It was the first time that I had ever experienced any depression at all. I struggled so much during this time of my life. I was working full time, raising 2 kids, and pregnant with my 3rd with severe depression, anxiety/panic attacks and insomnia. I was afraid to seek out professional help so I did a great job hiding this from everyone. Only my immediate family and a few friends were aware of it.

Please seek out professional help if you are struggling with any mental health issues, I am sure my experience would have been a lot more manageable, had I done that. This experience further separated my husband and I as he didn't even know how to respond to the new me. The more I looked to him for love and comfort the more he pushed me away. I was able to get through this time in my life with the help of a few friends that were available to me for emotional support 24 hours a day. And when I say, '24 hours a day", I am not exaggerating. I want to take the time to thank those friends of mine who had a whole lot of sleepless nights with me. I appreciate you and I want you to know that your unconditional love and support for me during that difficult time helped me heal and pull through to the other side.

In January of 2015, I gave birth to my 3rd beautiful baby girl. The next few years were tough, as I focused solely on being a mom and I disconnected from myself and my husband. During that time I felt alone, sad, unfulfilled, and stuck. I was blaming everyone else for all of my troubles and by 'everyone', I mean my husband. Everything was his fault and I was just an innocent bystander. I blamed him for everything and took responsibility for nothing, which is what led me to that one fateful day that I spoke about at the beginning of the story. Yes, that dramatic day when I fell to my knees, cried until my shirt was soaked with tears and my eyes were red and swollen. That was the day I took my power back. That was the day I miraculously knew that things were going to be okay, and most importantly, that was the day I made the decision to take responsibility for my life and to surrender to a higher power. On that day, I began my spiritual journey. A journey that led me to a brand new world of healing, discovery and possibilities.

'And what does that have to do with Collaboration?' you may ask. Well, everything. I've alway heard people say that when the student is ready the teacher will appear. Well, let's just say that's exactly how my spiritual journey began.

After that moment of heartfelt clarity and sweet surrender, I began to attract so many amazing spiritual teachers into my life, and those teachers helped me to connect with my deepest self. I started to shine light and accept all of the pieces of me, yes by 'all' I mean all (even the pieces of me that once brought me fear and shame). I brought light to those parts of me with so much love and compassion, and I forgave all of the people and circumstances in my life that had once held me back. But most importantly, I forgave myself. Forgiving myself and others was one of the hardest things that I had to do in my journey but, that was the most liberating experience of my life. By forgiving the past, I was able to release all of those circumstances and people in my life that were subconsciously weighing me down. During my healing journey, I realized that those people could only do things to the best of their awareness and that hurt people hurt people not because they want to hurt them, but because they are hurting themselves and they are just trying to survive the best way they know how.

You see, we are all desperate for love and desperate to be accepted, but we want to do this with our hearts completely closed off, and this is not possible. As long as we keep our hearts closed, we won't be able to connect to others, our environment and most importantly ourselves. By opening up my heart, I was able to connect to myself with authenticity and vulnerability, and from a place of unconditional love and compassion.

When you start to view the world from this angle and from this perspective, life truly becomes magical because that is when you clearly begin to see that we are all one and connected. This is when you start to truly trust yourself and when you trust yourself, you trust others. When you trust others, you trust your environment and when you trust your environment, you begin to trust in the unknown. When you trust in the unknown, you trust in possibilities. When you trust in possibilities, you trust in a higher power. When you trust in a higher power, you live your life with joy, faith and freedom. So the joy, peace and freedom that you have been searching for your entire life is laying dormant deep within you, waiting for you to discover it, nurture it and release it.

You and I come from the same divine power/source and if I can do it, you can do it too. I challenge you to take that trip deep into your soul, to really have the courage to find your power and use it. Your power will not only transform your life, but also the lives of the people around you and therefore, the world. And that, my dear friends, is what I like to call COLLABORATION.

Here is a quick exercise to help you get you out of your head/ego and into your heart. Close your eyes, place one hand over your heart and one over your belly and take about 6-9 slow and deep belly breaths. This exercise will help calm your nervous system and move you from stress/anxiety to peace and calmness in the present moment. It will help you move from fear and into love in just a few short minutes.

I fully believe in you because I know who you are and where you came from. Do you believe in you???

Thank you for going down this journey with me, I appreciate you.

If you would like a taste of my work, get my free workbook "*5 Steps to Begin Manifesting your Dreams*" here: https://divinegrowthcoaching.com

To book your special launch price session go here: https://calendly.com/divinegrowthcoaching/collaboration-launch-special-one-on-one-session

ABOUT THE AUTHOR

ARMIDA ABREU MARTINEZ

Armida Abreu Martínez is a Life & Relationship Coach located in Massachusetts helping clients nationwide who are going through deep and painful insecurities as well as relationship struggles and hardships. Armida obtained her Love and Authenticity Certificate from Authentic Living, where she learned how to facilitate internal healing by uncovering and addressing the root causes of external symptoms. Additionally, she earned her NLP Certification from the Association for Integrative Psychology which is helping her serve her clients with overcoming limiting beliefs, breaking behavioral patterns, creating more freedom & choice over their mindset, and developing stronger and healthier relationships. Her mission is to help people remove fear based living through healing, self-acceptance and unconditional love. Her vision is for humanity to move beyond fear and separation and into love and oneness.

Contact details:
Email: armida@divinegrowthcoaching.com
Website: https://divinegrowthcoaching.com
Facebook: https://www.facebook.com/divinegrowthcoachingservices
Instagram: https://www.instagram.com/divinegrowthcoaching/
YouTube: https://www.youtube.com/channel/UC-mv-q8MZGWc_po_1yaXqUQ

CINDY D CERECER

COLLABORATION WITH SELF

I THINK I SHOULD START BY INTRODUCING MYSELF.

My name is Cindy Cerecer. I'm a mum of 4 and a leader in Colon Hydrotherapy and the Natural Health industry. I run a Wellness Clinic in Melbourne as well as a Training Academy and Professional Association for Colon Hydrotherapists. Bit of a "niche market" I know, but I feel like in some way the industry chose me, rather than me choosing the industry.

In this chapter I am going to write about collaboration with self. This is a topic that really does excite me. There is nothing more powerful than looking at your shit, taking responsibility for your shit and realising that all the shit that you see externally is a manifestation of YOUR OWN SHIT that you are still holding on to. Collaboration with self is the epitome of all collaborations—because the world around us is simply a projection of who we believe ourselves to be.

The next thing you need to know about me is that I am a Scorpio. I don't actually know anything about horoscopes, but an astrologer once told me that Scorpios don't mind working with shit. I thought she was making light conversation about my career choice, but what she was really trying to say is that Scorpios are ok with holding space and leaning into the "messier stuff". They are brave and are always the first to volunteer themselves for difficult tasks. The kind of people that slow the car down and look out the window at a car crash—pimple poppers—that's a Scorpio.

Scorpios are also truth-seekers and painfully honest - sometimes even to their own detriment. That's also me. I was born with the ability to see through the bullshit, which, ironically, didn't make things easier for me; it actually made growing up extremely difficult. Even as a very young child, I was different. I triggered people. I was outspoken and I constantly felt uncomfortable with the idea that "this was all that there was."

I longed to just be like everyone else, to just be ok with the status quo; particularly when I was very young—I just couldn't filter it. Probably due to the fact that I had the need to share my opinion on EVERYTHING, I felt like I was always getting in trouble and being asked to change, to buffer myself and to make myself more socially digestible. This led to many futile attempts to fit in, to feel accepted and understood for who I was.

"Why can't you just be like so-and-so?" was a question I remember hearing often.

So naturally this led me into having an extremely complicated relationship with myself. I felt that love was conditional. Nothing I ever did was good enough. I was never "enough". Depression and anxiety spiraled into an eating disorder, and life inside my head during my teenage years was pretty fucked-up. Nevertheless there is always beauty in the madness. Moving through that experience is probably one of the things that I am most proud of. It was a wonderful journey of digging deep to get to know myself on a level that I had never experienced. From discovery, I could move to acceptance and from acceptance, things blossomed into collaboration.

Recovery from Anorexia has taught me such a profound synergy and coherence with myself and who I truly am—and that which I am not —that I am left with nothing but gratitude and respect for that time in my life.

The good news is that I have since become unapologetically content with just being me. I'm definitely the black sheep of the family—the one that collects crystals, eats organic and thinks she can cure everything with colonics, vegetable juice, essential oils and a few deep breaths. (No ... but seriously ... you can.) Be that as it may, I no longer seek validation or acceptance from anything that is external like family, friends, society, etc. It's now an inside job, so to speak. My relationship with myself has evolved into a fun game that I play inside my head to see how often I can disrupt the matrix.

The true beauty of this is that because my collaboration with myself and my own internal dialogue, belief systems and programing—what I fundamentally believe—creates my reality, (and this is something that I hold true, intrinsically, on every level of my being) it manifests externally into my life without me even trying. Cool eh? I'll write more on this a little later.

Why have we lived for so long in a society of competition and comparison? The answer is simple: because like attracts like. It's all we have ever seen, so it's the only example we have ever had to follow.

Greg Braden puts it so powerfully in the first chapter of his book, The Science of Self Empowerment: *"Everything from our self esteem to our self worth, our sense of confidence, our well-being, and our sense of safety, as well as the way we see the world and other people, stems from our answer to the question WHO ARE WE?"*

Let's think critically for a minute. Western culture really doesn't spend much time educating us on who we are or where we came from. Big Bang, Evolution and Death are the 3 main principles that are supposed to explain our existence, and anything that hasn't been "proven by science" is completely discredited.

Most of us were born into the consciousness of the Illusion of separation. The mind/ego tells us, "I am me and you are you. Therefore we are separate from each other." The illusion of separation creates insecurity. Insecurity creates judgement as we start to compare ourselves to each other, to see who is better, luckier, smarter, prettier, more desirable—and so the illusion continues.

Most of us critical thinkers have already met with the disenchantment of the structures and systems that surround us. Science is funded by large corporations selling us products that make us sick so we can go get medicine that the corporations themselves sell. Blah blah blah.

So without a fundamental understanding of who we truly are and where we come from, we are doomed to fall into the illusion as a default setting. This leads to feelings of emptiness and perhaps even depression as we lack connection with others—because fundamentally we lack connection with ourselves. How can one connect with something that you have no idea what it is?

However, consciousness is shifting. The veil is thinning. People are waking up and we are starting to see the stories that the mind creates. That's all they are. Stories, narratives, illusions—not truths.

I have no doubt that if you are reading this it's because you feel it too. That feeling that there has to be more—that there has to be a better way—that the old paradigm just doesn't add up.

The human mind by design makes illusions, just like a toaster makes toast. These illusions can be fun, exciting and entertaining. (I bet you're enjoying reading this book, aren't you? Yes that's part of the illusion as well.) But sometimes these illusions DO NOT serve us. They are disempowering. They create fear. They have a lower vibrational frequency. They can even make us sick—that's when one has to remember that the mind is only a tool—and if there are no nails and no wood, you need to put your bloody hammer away!!

The illusion of separation no longer serves us. We have shifted—times have changed and we are moving into a collective consciousness of oneness and collaboration. Synchronicity and connection—this is how we change the world, folks,—SO TAKE NOTES—but firstly and fundamentally we need to heal and consolidate our collaboration with ourselves. That's what got me so excited and grateful to be able to share my story in this chapter.

So let me go back to a time when all I knew was illusions.

I actually remember the day quite vividly—the day when I literally realised that I had absolutely no idea who I was. I was 21, living in Mexico, engaged to my now husband and living underneath a mango tree in this tiny little apartment that we

affectionately called "la depa". Life was good, I was happy and my struggles with my eating disorder were no longer as violent as they had been when I was a teenager. I was winning. I had things under control.

I was sitting at my computer, a lime-green HP laptop, using "MySpace". MySpace was like an earlier version of Facebook where you could create your own profile and share things like photos and music that you liked. Anyway, the platform had prompted me because I hadn't filled out my profile questions. So I clicked the link to a series of questions that I was supposed to answer. Name, Age, Relationship Status, Likes, Dislikes, Hobbies, Favorite things, etc. etc. Now this wasn't the first time I had had to fill in something like this, but for some reason this time was different.

All of a sudden it hit me. I started to experience anxiety, I became fidgety, restless, and waves of emotions began pouring in. I sobbed as my hands shook, unable to type the answers into my keyboard. I had a realization that any previous answer that I had ever given to those questions was a people pleasing answer. An answer that screamed

"Please love me, because I love the same music as you", "Please accept me, because I like doing whatever you like doing." Every single decision I had ever made in my life was made in a useless bid not to disappoint others.

I honestly had no idea what I liked, because I had spent my whole life trying to fit in by pretending to like whatever I thought everybody else liked. So desperate to be loved, that I would do everything that I thought everyone else would have loved me for doing. So scared that people would dislike me that I never disliked anything that I thought anybody else would like.

Now this wasn't my first epiphany on my road to my eating disorder recovery. I had had many. One of the most poignant ones was when I realised that everybody was so worried about what others thought of them that they weren't really focusing on me anyway. Another realisation that I had was that I couldn't really control or predict what other people would think or feel, and I really had no idea about what was going on inside someone else's head. I mean no one had any idea of the irrational nightmare that was constantly spinning around in my head, so how was I supposed to know what was going on in theirs?

These discoveries were quite liberating for me and enabled me to have the fortitude to say, "STUFF IT! I may not know who I am, but I'm going to create who I want to be right here and now!" So after composing myself from my blubbering mess I mustered up the courage to answer each and every question, filling in each text box with responses that felt true for me right there and then in the moment.

For the first time in 21 years I had consciously created my own identity. It took about 30 minutes as I made decisions about what music I liked, hobbies I enjoyed doing, and the three items I'd take with me if I ever became stranded on a deserted island. I may have only filled out a MySpace profile but I felt like I had conquered Everest.

I feel like that marked the beginning of something truly life changing for me. Of course I had read books and affirmations about loving and accepting myself and yadda yadda yadda, but how on Earth was I going to do that without ever knowing truly who I was, or at least giving myself permission to be whoever or whatever I felt like being?

As soon as I had let go of being worried about what others thought, letting anybody down, upsetting or disappointing other people, I literally opened the floodgates to an exciting journey of self discovery, constant re-creation, and most importantly, collaboration.

I spent many years of reflection looking back on that story from la depa, trying to pinpoint what it was that pushed me to that space of wanting to know myself better. What was it that allowed me to open to something deeper? Why was it in that moment, or at that time of my life that I was able to realise that this was my next step in personal growth?

A few years earlier I had switched to a plant based diet and eliminated all animal products. It was actually a doctor who told me to become vegetarian, which led me down a path of research on plant-based diets. From what I read, I decided that veganism made sense to me, so I gave it a go.

I spent my nights on vegan forums and chat groups trying to find recipes and different ways to make sure I was eating a balanced diet. Funnily enough, "vegans" were very into colon cleansing. There were many interesting posts about the health benefits of cleansing your colon, getting rid of parasites and how to do your own at-home enemas.

I had always had gut issues like constipation and IBS but I never thought that there was anything I could do about it. I just thought that was the way my body was and that I was genetically destined to have a slow gut. One day, I was in a pharmacy in California. I saw an enema kit for sale, bought it, and started to do my own enemas.

Doing enemas was quite a revelation. Not only did it help me with my gut issues, it gave me a sense of calmness that I had never had. I was no longer worried about "how my tummy would feel" because I knew I could immediately fix it with an enema if need be. Little did I know that I had made a discovery that would lead me down a giant rabbit hole of self discovery and collaboration.

Leaning to heal my gut, trust my gut, and follow my gut instinct has now grown into a career where I not only help others with their own personal journeys, but I train some of the best Colon Hydrotherapists Internationally and help them open their own Colon Hydrotherapy Clinics that, in turn, change hundreds of thousands of lives.

I must say that this is something that I am very proud of.

The way I see it is, we are all full of shit. It's part of the human condition. The process of looking at your shit, knowing and understanding it, then learning how to either let go of what's not serving you or integrate what is needed is one of the most empowering and liberating tools one can ever learn. This is what COLLABORATION WITH SELF means to me: To know how to get your shit sorted.

Leaning to be ok with, and processing your "messy stuff" is, for me, what colonics are all about.

Many people say to me when they come into the clinic, "how the hell did you end up doing this for a living?" It's a question that always makes me smile because for me colonics are about so much more than just poo. The spiritual and emotional revelations that come with holding space for clients as they go on this amazing journey of cleaning their digestive tract is what keeps me so inspired and passionate about the industry.

When one finally chooses to let go of old crap that no longer serves them, it brings them one step closer to who they truly are—and one step further away from their illusions and delusions.

So many emotions get stored in the gut too. Anger, trauma, fear, confusion are the main ones—but the body is so amazing it will find a way to "protect" us from anything we think might harm us. Ironically, holding on to emotions will cause illness in the body. Releasing what we no longer need creates space and energy for us to grow and thrive.

At Colonic Care we guide our clients through a process we call "10 in 30". 10 colonics within 30 days. This allows the treatments to cleanse deep into the bowel, releasing old stagnant waste and parasites, and at the same time, it exercises the colon and stimulates new muscle memory through peristalsis. The process is truly transformational.

It is recommended that you set a clear intention—physically, mentally, emotionally, AND spiritually for the cleanse. We ask our clients to focus on the habits and patterns that they are ready to let go of and make a list of the new programming and thoughts that they are ready to welcome in. It's like a spring clean for the body, mind, and soul.

Not all Colon Hydrotherapists are trained in, or familiar with this holistic process of "10 in 30" so it's recommended that you seek out an ICHTA (International Colon Hydrotherapy Training Academy) Certified Colon Hydrotherapist and Clinic to guide you through this process. www.ichta.org

I have also founded ICHA (International Colon Hydrotherapy Association). ICHA has just released an app with courses available for those wanting to do a "10 in 30" journey, learn more about colonics, or even train to be a colon hydrotherapist. https://icha.passion.io

Thank you for allowing me to share my journey through this chapter. It has been an honor to be involved in such a beautiful collaboration. When we 'cut the crap', so to speak, we are finally acknowledging who we truly are and getting rid of what we are not. Stories, illusions, trapped emotions - all stop us from remembering the truth: That we are all one, and that all is connected.

By embracing and collaborating with all aspects of yourself, you are opening yourself up to embrace and collaborate with others. This is the true foundation of the new Earth.

ABOUT THE AUTHOR

CINDY D CERECER

Cindy D Cerecer knows her SHIT! Not only is she a mum of 4, but she is a leader in the Colon Hydrotherapy Industry and a Holistic Health Expert.

Cindy is the owner of Colonic Care in Melbourne Australia, The Principal of ICHTA (International Colon Hydrotherapy Training Academy) and the President of ICHA (International Colon Hydrotherapy Association). She is a Certified Holistic Nutritionist, Life Coach and Theta Healer. She recently received a grant from the University of Natural Health in Indianapolis to complete their PHD Programs in Holistic Health, Healing and Medicine.

Holistic Health means happiness and health of the mind, body and soul. Cindy utilises colonics to work on a physical level to shift stagnant waste from the body, but combined with spiritual and energy practices one can master the clearing of the mind and stagnant beliefs that are no longer serving us.

Her chapter in this book is all about COLLABORATION WITH SELF. —A lighthearted but sincere guide to facing one's 💩 and getting it sorted!

Clinic: www.coloniccare.com.au
Training Academy: www.ichta.org

Association: https://icha.passion.io
Facebook: www.facebook.com/coloniccare
Email: cindy@coloniccare.com

JAYNE MARQUIS

BEING YOUR AUTHENTIC VERSION OF SELF TO CONTRIBUTE TO THE MASTERPIECE OF THE "WHOLE"

INTRODUCTION

Consider this. The spiral is ubiquitous in nature. It is everywhere, all around us, part of us. Our blood spirals out of our hearts, our very DNA is in the shape of a spiral. In nature, it's found in seashells, pinecones, flowers, fiddleheads, snails, whirlpools, hurricanes, tornadoes, galaxies, to name a few. It represents growth, evolution and change. The spiral represents the slow reveal of what is hidden. It means coming back to a place more expanded but with a deeper understanding. The spiral reminds us that we are constantly evolving, body, mind, and soul.

We have understood how to spiral up as a whole in the past, we have somehow strayed in our desire to have more, be more, to rule and conquer, our God has often been competition, and greed.

A different way has been known; the African people call it Ubuntu - "authentic individual human beings are part of a larger and more significant relational, communal, societal, environmental and spiritual world". True collaboration begins with loving ourselves completely, being our whole authentic magnificent selves, by acting, being in the now, and trusting that prosperity will be the result.

Perhaps we have been on a journey, perhaps many times, spiraling around the sun, in order to get a greater understanding of true collaboration. It is time, the rotation has happened, we are at the point where we can be something greater. We can realize as we have made the grand circle, that a more expanded, deeper collaboration is needed in order to truly thrive.

MY STORY

If you had told me when I was 12 that I would be a naturopathic doctor, a homeopath, a Canadian ballroom dance champ, a pilot, an equestrian, a podcast host, a published author, and a collaborator with some of the most beautiful people on the planet, I would never have believed it. Life was confusing, emotional, and hard when I was a child. But perhaps that was the momentum, the catalyst that I needed to follow my excitement, to act on my intuition and walk through the doors that opened.

My childhood was tough, not because of lack of "things", "food", or "shelter", but because of what felt like a whirlpool of confusion, a feeling that I wasn't wanted in the community. I felt shunned. This was difficult, especially when all a child wants is to belong. It felt harsh and turbulent. I felt unheard, not seen, like I didn't matter. In hindsight, I understand that what happened was because of lack of collaboration and a belief that in order to have abundance you had to tower over someone else, keep them small, and draw attention to yourself. At a very early age I began to question what life was all about. I turned to books and the masters, and I turned inward for the answers. This inward journey for answers led me to become the best version of myself. It is now my belief that when we become the best version of ourselves, our authentic selves, when we master our own individual gifts and talents, that life moves us in the right direction. The universe hears our call, and if we listen to the answers we know what is next. Life unfolds and we find our place, adding our completeness to the whole. True Collaboration.

When I was very young, well actually before I was born, my mother had just graduated from University. She lived in a very small town, but she was strong and determined to do something special in this world, to make her contribution. She had entrepreneurial instincts and convinced her father that she could retail the woolen goods he was manufacturing, instead of just wholesaling them. He was certain no one would drive to a small town to purchase woolen blankets and socks from a small room beside a woolen mill, but he let her start. The collaboration began. Unfortunately, it was doomed to failure. Not because of lack of success, but because of success.

My grandfather had grown up during the great depression. He craved success, money, property, and status to be what society called "successful". He wanted what my mother had created all for himself.

What happened as this very unlikely business grew to become successful? Collaboration and more growth? A search to find room for each to contribute to the whole? My grandfather proudly allowing my mother the room and place to grow and become the best, most beautiful version of herself?

Sadly, no. My grandfather wanted to be in control and take back ownership in totality. He got his wealth, his Rolls Royce, his status, his fame in a small town. But he lost his family and collaboration became impossible.

In this era that, hopefully, we are vibrating out of, success is defined by what we see on TV and in movies. It is the large house, the ability to travel on planes, yachts, to have prestige, perhaps a famous album, to be a rockstar, a movie star, a model. I have learned to call this the programming of our time. And now I see it for what it is. I did not know this back then. And clearly my grandfather followed the mantra. Why else would he want it all? However, honestly, without him, I would not be who I am today, so I am grateful.

My grandfather made a humble living, he was good at what he did. He had a home and a family. But what goes wrong when we lack the trust that there is enough abundance for all, when we stop collaboration in fear that we won't be the most important, the richest, the one to have control of it all? Could it be that we are seeing this as a people on a larger scale? We see the rape of Mother Earth to have endless wealth, the call for green taxes that keep us dependent when the technology for free energy already exists. We hear of the need to depopulate when perhaps we need to come together and find the answers.

Why? To keep humanity small and enslaved to a system in order to have control, money, people, and things?

So it is a story of our time, a universal one, one that we must spiral out of. It has made me ponder, to question, at least since I was 12.

There is a time in each of us when we need to make a choice. Stay small, stay a lesser version of ourselves in order to stay "safe", "accepted", what someone else wants us to be. Or we grow. We become our best selves, we remember why we came. Often this choice involves complete separation so that the lid cannot be placed on our dreams so that we can make our own choices, so that we can thrive. This is the path my mother chose. She chose to break free, she left, owning nothing, taking nothing but her spirit and drive to create. She left to start again.

QUESTION EVERYTHING

Nothing would be simple for me ever again. I had started my journey of questioning.

Why are we kept small for the benefit of others?

What if we are successful? Must we hoard and keep it all? Keep our secrets, lest it all be stolen and taken from us? It happens!! Why? Do some feel they don't have their own unique brilliance to contribute, so they have to steal it from others?

Why are we kept sick for the benefit of others, for profit? Could this be?

When does programming start that makes us believe having great wealth or fame will make us happy? And where did these ideas come from?

When did the programming start that health comes in a pill, that someone else is our savior, that healing is something outside of ourselves?

Later after becoming a naturopathic doctor, I asked, "why is my patient afraid to tell me they are seeing another health care practitioner? Are they afraid I will insist it is only me that they can see? That I will fire them, or act from an ego state, insisting only I have the answers. Are they afraid I won't help them if they wish to move on their own path? Is this their experience here?"

Are the answers already available to allow humanity to flourish? Free energy, the cure for cancer and other diseases, why are they not revealed? To keep us small and sick for profit?

And, what about the opposite? if we desire nothing, will we be happy then?

What if we choose to do nothing, and then if someone else is successful they should give us part of their success. Is this the answer? Or is it a different form of slavery? Another way to keep us small, inert?

What If we take without giving? Do we lose a sense of who we are? Does this too conspire to keep us incomplete?

And the big question:Why do we go to school, to college, universities, to become slaves to this system? Wait, are we slaves? To whom? Who is collaborating to make this so?

And could it be that the pain and turmoil that I experienced as a child was my biggest gift? Do we come here in a state of amnesia of the knowledge of who we truly are? Through the trials of life we could possibly wake to it?

We live in a fractal world. In hindsight, I see that my story is a fractal of what I believe is going on on a much larger scale. To heal the world we need to heal ourselves. We must remember why we came, that we have a unique mission that if found will contribute to the whole. We must remember how powerful we are, and that we belong to a much greater whole. To change the world, first, change must happen within ourselves. We are the ones. We are the change, it all starts within each of us.

CHANGE, EMPOWERMENT, COLLABORATION, AND HEALING IS AN INSIDE JOB

I didn't know it, but my journey to become a naturopathic doctor and a homeopath probably began at that time of difficulty, when I was 12. It was then that I could see the only way out was to go inside for understanding. Somehow I knew that it was this place inside me where I could find my connection to the "all", to the answers, to the "Oneness". My reaction to what was going on outwardly was to go inward. And so I learned to meditate. I read many books about spirituality and philosophy. I was fortunate that my mother had a bookshelf-full, (she too was looking for answers).

Later I read Bruce Lipton's "*The Biology of Belief*" . He made me realize that our thoughts have a direct effect on our physical bodies. I read Barbara Brennan's book "*Hands of Light*". A NASA scientist who could see the human energy field, she showed how our thoughts, our emotions, and what we consumed all affected our energetic bodies, and that these, in turn, affected the physical. What I saw was how complex, beautiful and powerful we are.

My journey to becoming a naturopathic doctor took time because it meant withdrawing support for my mother's business which had become successful again. I had stayed in our family business for a few years. In this time, with my husband we became Canadian ballroom dance champions and got our pilot's licenses. Life was full and rewarding.

But when the Universe calls you to your destiny, especially if you have asked, (And I had asked. Deep down I knew we all come with a soul purpose and gift to bring to this world.) a time comes when it is time to discover this, whenall that exists seems to stall. It loses its sparkle or becomes impossible to continue as is. With me, business became difficult; it was like moving through quicksand. As it became more and more difficult (the wake-up call) it became obvious that I wasn't following my calling, my reason for being here. And once again the catalyst was discomfort and pain.

So one afternoon, and I remember it as if it was yesterday, I got on my knees and asked my higher self to reveal what it was that I came here to do. I knew it was time. The next day while walking my dog, in nature, of a quiet mind, I simply heard, "you should be a doctor". I was more than surprised, it had never even occurred to me. But when one asks and listens, change can happen very fast. I heard the voice inside me whisper, I felt the excitement, and so I moved into action. I knew what resonated, and I was enrolled and was studying within 6 weeks to become a naturopathic doctor, at CCNM in Toronto, Canada. One of the most difficult studies of my life began. It was a 4-year comprehensive, grueling course.

Simultaneously, my dance career was over, as I was pregnant with twins! I must add, my husband was my dance partner, my business partner, my partner in life, and the collaboration with him is a whole other story of support and sync.

There was a twinge of sadness. I loved so much of what we were doing, but change requires us to let go of the riverbank of safety when we hear the call. Life can spiral quickly at such times, and it wasn't going to be easy. But you know what? When you know in your heart that you are on the right path, you dig deep and nothing can stop you. And so, I studied harder with newborn twins, than I ever had in my life.

In my second year at CCNM, I went to India with the school to learn from the masters about homeopathy. It was on this trip that I realized homeopathy would be my passion. It was one of the modalities that we studied as an ND. I was intrigued with it because it took into account the physical symptoms, but even more importantly to me, it was true mind-body medicine. It looked at the person as a whole. It saw disease as a stuck state of energy that was often tied into programming and beliefs that no longer served. It listened to the body as a mirror of what was going on in the mind. And then, with a remedy made from nature, it worked at a deep energetic level. Its philosophy is to treat the whole person, and to treat "like with like". Homeopathy is an ever-evolving collaborative health system. It was everything that resonated with me. I went on and studied 3 more years to become a homeopath at OCHM.

My second life into healing and empowering myself with knowledge and encouraging others to do the same had begun. I was becoming the reason I came to this planet. It has all formed me, my early years, the pain, the separation, learning, dancing, flying, business. Every bit of my life made me who I was. I knew how to dig deep, to find the power within, to have a passion, and move toward it. To lean into the good, the bad, and just show up. What I didn't know was that the fractal would show up once again in my passion. Again the questions and the aggravation with the state of this planet loomed.

It came when I realized that homeopathy was not embraced by traditional medicine as we know it. As I pursued my passion, I didn't know this. I was excited and determined to master this beautiful philosophy and medicine. I experienced time and time again that it worked. And so again I questioned. Why does allopathic medicine attack what it does not understand? Why does it not collaborate and look at homeopathy with curiosity? Why did it make it seem that it couldn't work? Was it once again for profit and control? To keep it small, so another can reign supreme? As it turns out, nature can't be patented. Only variations of nature. So homeopathy is far from lucrative, and from what I've seen, it is far too healing. I was shocked by the attacks. Horrified, to be honest. When you are completely aware of the good in something, and it comes under attack, you have to question why, and with my background, it was far too obvious.

The desire to keep us small, to keep us from truly healing, from becoming our best self is a desire to control. It is top-down domination. It allows huge profit for those in power. It stops imagination, communion with nature, a belief in ourselves, and in our own inner power. True healing comes when we collaborate with those of wisdom and caring but then go inside to commune with ourselves and the answers that come. To be the final choice-makers in our own healing, and to be responsible, ultimately, for our own path. The programming over several decades to believe in a savior outside ourselves has made it easy to control us. As my story tells, true collaboration is impossible when something tries to dominate. We must find a way to remember who we are.

WHAT I HAVE COME TO KNOW AS UNIVERSAL TRUTH.

1. The answers lie in each of us. As we desire to find our purpose for being, it will be revealed. We must ask.

2. Self-love needs to be mastered. As we learn to love ourselves we can connect to our heart which in turn is connected to the Unified Field of oneness. When we connect to the unified field the most amazing, brilliant heart-centered answers come. Doors open and it is here that the answers to our questions lie, and where true genius lives.

3. As we become our unique, whole, incredible selves, doors open, growth happens; we are asked to act. Our actions are our response to

the Universe. And more is revealed. When we act there is also a momentum that starts a movement toward change. If we stagnate, often there is a catalyst to evolve.

4. As we listen, and as we take action, the spiral continues to unfold and true collaboration can happen. If we trust in our own power, our unique essence, our spark, our connection to something much greater than ourselves, we can be a part of a much larger whole that will constantly evolve into something far more beautiful than we can even imagine. The answers lie in each of us. We are the ones.

AS I EVOLVE.

1. Podcast

As I saw the programming push to forget all these things I responded by asking what is next. I started a podcast: *INpowered Mind, INpowered Health*. A podcast meant to be INspiration to empower and awaken a deep knowledge that we are magnificent and powerful. The spiral symbolizes our journey, returning to the same place, but expanded. Our mind influences our health, our state, our future. Information is the keystone to empowerment. Belief is the keystone for transformation. I have powerful conversations with beautiful people inspiring us to be our best selves in mind and in health. We are the ones. A reminder with every episode to look INside to "Spiral up, spiral out" - It is Mind-Body INspiration. You will find the link in my biography.

2. Jayne's INpowered Handbook

I also wrote a book, "*Jayne's INpowered Handbook*". Explaining how to use 17 homeopathic remedies and 12 Tissue Salts, successfully. It is meant to take the mystery out of dosing and choosing a remedy when every day small healing challenges happen. Bone breaks, concussions, flu, bug bites, and more. It's meant to be a first step in empowering yourself with information to help heal. As you gain confidence in this small way, and use this medicine successfully you will empower yourself with more and expanded knowledge. It is meant to be a catalyst to learning all about homeopathy and tissue salts. You can find the link in my biography.

3. Course

I'm also working on an INpowering online course *"J.U.M.P Journeying To Understand my Power"*. It's meant to move all of us into the magical space of remembering who we truly are: strong, whole, and empowered. I began to create this course in my twenties in response to others who were like me, hurt and unsure of how to live this life. Forgetful of the knowledge, that true inspiration and deep knowing comes from inside. Its focus is on teenagers, but helps remind anyone to become the best version of themselves in order to truly collaborate and contribute to the whole. Let's be the Ones. Let's be the change. Let's remember. Let's spiral into true collaboration.

And become INpowered.

ABOUT THE AUTHOR

JAYNE MARQUIS

Dr. Jayne Marquis (ND., HOM) is a Naturopathic Doctor, Homeopath, and Podcast Host of INpowered Mind INpowered Health. She achieved her diploma to become a Naturopathic Doctor at the Canadian College of Naturopathic Medicine. Here she learned to become a Doctor but then treat with Natural Medicine. She learned Chinese medicine, Acupuncture, Botanical Medicine, Massage, Nutrition, Orthomolecular medicine, and Homeopathy.

It was homeopathy that resonated, because of the mind-body connection. She went on to become a Homeopath at the Ontario College of Homeopathic Medicine and has studied with some of the best homeopaths in the world.

Jayne's desire to awaken people to their own inner power and recognize the connection between mind, body, and spirit and then connect to their own ability to find true health resulted in her international podcast "INpowered Mind, INpowered Health" Follow link tree below to find it on 12 platforms.

She is the author of "Jayne's INpowered Handbook" published recently, teaching about the 12 Schuessler cell salts and 17 homeopathic remedies.

Today, Jayne wholeheartedly continues to guide herself and others toward empowerment, knowledge, inner discovery, and health. Her mission is to inspire everyone to become INpowered.

For Jayne's free ebook: The INpowering benefits of homeopathy and Tissue salts:
Website: INpoweredhealth.com/freebie
Facebook link: https://www.facebook.com/inpoweredmind
Website and Podcast link: https://inpoweredhealth.com/books/
My Linktree: https://linktr.ee/INpoweredhealth
Inpowered Handbook: https://books.friesenpress.com/store/title/119734000015173095

JENNIFER ACKAD

UNAPOLOGETICALLY AUTHENTIC: COLLABORATING WITH YOUR TRUE SELF TO EMBODY YOUR DEEPEST DESIRES AND LIVE IN ALIGNMENT WITH YOUR HIGHEST CALLING

THE KNOWING OF THE HEART

We all have a unique colour to reveal. Each one of us is designed in a very unique way, and are born with gifts that are meant to be shared with the world. When we are in true collaboration with ourselves first, we allow our intrinsic light to shine and serve its purpose. That is when we really serve our planet and are able to collaborate with others.

There is a beautiful potential in each one of us, waiting to be seen, acknowledged and unleashed, one step at a time.

Imagine the ripple effects on our collective if each one of us would take responsibility for the jewels we hold within. Imagine the impact it could have on the collective love, joy and on the frequency of our planet.

When we choose to own up to the potential that is inside of us, to live by what is genuinely true for us, our energy is at its most efficient and has direct influence on the 'big picture'. We choose to collaborate with others in flow, truth and harmony, knowing that this flow, truth and harmony is tasted within first.

When *'The Authentic Woman You Are'* platforms came to life, my soul was crying for this alignment. I had been immersed in a very profound journey in a yoga school for 9 years, and my longing was to see all our group and tribe rise in collaboration, all in our light and gifts, all serving in the authentic life design we were meant to have. The longing in my heart was sincere, but the set up was not the right one to manifest this calling for me then. Strong forces and currents made me jump out of there with great faith, trust and surrender, and there it was. I was ready to be reborn. I gathered 23 women speakers for a summit series on a platform to share their gifts, light and stories with the world. A platform where there was no competition or comparaison, but a sincere desire to share ourselves and the messages we held, embodied in the voice and vibration that were ready to express.

'We are all in this together'; I wanted to start living by that.

DISCOVERING HOME WITHIN

All my life I felt that there was a deeper way of living and was feeling called by it. I was always very sensitive and had the longing for real, profound and intimate connection. I was seeking for that place where I could feel safe, where I could feel home, where I could be all that I am with enthusiasm and without judgment.

When I made that jump out of the corporate world in 2010, I dove inside my body to explore, be curious and learn about how and what it was communicating. I was fascinated and it became a way of living, peeling off layers after layers to reconnect more and more to the nature and essence of the woman I was.

And what did I find?

...

Home within.

Home within is the treasure I found.

'I am going Home', this is what I had told my boss as I was leaving the engineering field.

I was scared, yes, but the intention was clear. Home was an unknown territory that I was reclaiming, I was going into an adventure to discover what home meant, I was jumping IN. And the jewels I found totally blew my mind. I was not expecting that world and without knowing it, it was the start of the best backpacking trip of my Life.

Our bodies hold the keys to a world of possibilities that are designed for us, for our lives and for the ripple effects it has on the life of others. It holds the whispers and the messages that are constantly guiding us to the next authentic step, and it's by paying attention to them that we align our lives in the most collaborative ways. Starting with Self.

When I started going 'in' and dove into the self-healing world, my body became my laboratory, my study land where I would learn directly from what was circulating inside of me. I became so passionate about it! My engineering logical mind dropped to feel and receive, and as I was feeling, my engineering skills were all there to innerstand and understand the system of this body and how it operated. How perfect! Combining two worlds!

Going deep inside requires courage, indeed, but then you know what?

It becomes a tool for life and you are 'home'.

What are you learning from your body?

What is your body showing you in terms of how it functions?

If you had to share about your inner experiences to someone else, how would it sound?

I am naming all of this to you not to turn you into teachers, but because this is how I learned profoundly.

I was sincere.

I was logging my practice everyday.

I was bringing intimate attention into my organs.

I was asking my body what it needed, I was collaborating with it and responding.

I was writing down the messages I was receiving from my tissues about my desires, my boundaries, my visions, my wounds, papa's voice, mama's voice, my survival habits/reactions/personas, etc.

Wow, a 'world' that I discovered.

Bringing presence to the body is the most valuable act of self-love we can do. When the body feels listened to, welcomed, acknowledged, given space to express, it starts revealing its secrets, and its gems come out. Just like a best friend who starts to share genuinely when feeling an authentic connection and a safe space to open without judgments, projections, preconceived ideas or expectations. Exactly the same.

We then start hearing the truth and wisdom of what it holds and that is priceless.

What is the number one ingredient to find home within and start releasing the potential we have inside?

Attention.

Attention is our true currency.

When we speak about home within, and about embodiment, it's all a matter of attention being 'in'.

Where is our attention?

Where is your attention now?

We are an anchored presence at the center of this embodied experience, and the inner world is a WHOLE world to discover and a dedication to embrace. It's the art of dis-identifying from all that we thought we were to welcome who we are intrinsically, who we are behind the survival reactions and mechanisms our bodies have been used to behave as. It's the art of tapping back into the true frequency of who we are, bringing attention to it and grounding in it.

Then our bodies start responding based on its true needs and boundaries, clarity is found, and our actions become ignited with meaning and freedom. The deeper answers propel us, putting aside one step at a time the compensations we have adopted based on a conditioned or experienced sense of danger. We go from feeling stuck in the surface version of ourselves to owning up to the next layer of authenticity ready to operate in our lives.

When I learned the art of listening within, I learned to unleash the trapped energy in my body, alchemize it into higher frequency and redirect it into purpose. I learned to activate my body and shift my attention leaks into reclaimed sovereignty and authentic power. I learned how to be intimate and connect with my body in a way that I had always dreamed about, releasing the old to welcome the new. And my desire is to share those tools with you.

Home within is simply magical and a sanctuary every person on earth should have access to. It opens us to receive from all that surrounds us, from the abundance that is, and helps us collaborate with one another with love, authenticity and deeply felt joy and freedom. And as we transform ourselves, we empower our lives and the lives of others.

FROM COMPETITION TO BEING IN OUR CREATIVE NATURE

Competition is an illusion. creativity is the key.

Competition comes from pushing, and is so tiring, but creativity comes from being—and it's life giving.

Growing up, I never really understood competition and always felt quite uncomfortable in it. For me, succeeding was about being total in an 'art', not about being better than another or even about achieving a goal, it was about the love of total presence in something that I was really into, about evolving and learning, and about being true. This is when I feel I am really winning.

When we love something with all of our body, heart and soul, we win, and it's effortless. We are carried by a flow that whispers and guides us into every step to take, every moment of the way.

But when we operate from the mind and expect a lot from ourselves, or allow expectations of others to dictate our behaviors, we lose; we feel trapped in 'how-to' or in 'performance' rather than operating from intuition or knowing, and there is no peace. We loop, we question ourselves: What must I do to be better? What must I do to be loved? What must I do to be acknowledged? What must I do to feel free?

We are designed with so much value, and it's a matter of saying yes to it.

The truth is, as we anchor in our deepest self, feeling safe to rest in who we truly are, our nervous system responds and allows us to be in our intrinsic and creative nature. We surrender to our value, to our purpose, to our calling, which is unique to us.

How can competition, jealousy and comparison appear in such a case?

They cannot!

When we are embodied in who we are, there is no room for those states of mind, but rather there is spaciousness in our being that allows us to serve with our energy and authentic power, whatever shape or form it takes.

We allow the force of love to ignite us and guide us.

What comes naturally to you?

What brings you gratitude and totality?

What are you really being called by?

Follow that road and you will win.

Surrendering into profound self-love helps us embody who we are born to be, not more, not less. It helps us embody our Godly given gifts and live our life through the lenses of our essence.

Then competition dissolves. Then all old structures and paradigms of separation dissolve, within and out, all that we are has its place. We see the beauty and perfect intelligence in all that exists, in collaboration and co-creation, living with intention, moment after moment.

Winning is about being unapologetically ourselves, and realizing that the biggest gift we give to others is to be 100% ourselves, the most authentic version of ourselves.

There is so much happening in our lives, so many structures and systems we opt into, that we have somehow learned that the 'norm' is to give our power to external grids and stop trusting our inner knowing, inner guidance and intuition. We have learned to operate inauthentically in order to feel safe in a system that promises to keep us safe. But what if safety was something completely different than what we have learned? What if safety was our birthright and that we are only safe by reclaiming our creative power?

FROM THE PATH OF ALONENESS TO COMING TOGETHER

My heart has always known that collaboration held the keys to so much more impact and joy in the world, but yet my body was programmed to feel alone, isolated and safer being able to 'do it on my own'.

I was born two months prematurally and had to be carried out into an incubator far from my parents, and from touch for several weeks. I was feeling alone.

I gave birth to my son in a context where my marriage was falling apart, and where my family was being quite challenged by my life choices. I was feeling alone.

I left the yoga tribe around which my life was centered, facing deep fears of being more visible with the gifts I had to share with the world. I was feeling alone.

And so many other examples.

Coming together is a path and collaboration is a journey.

In ideal it sounds nice, but in reality it asks for deep commitment and self-knowledge.

It asks for great response-ability.

A responsibility of both our shadow and our light, of both our limitations and wounds, and also acknowledgment of our power.

Really great collaborations require also great humility and vulnerability, to realize when we are vibrating lack rather than trust, or vibrating doubt, rather than courage.

It requires us to address the sincere values we hold and the direction our heart wants to follow.

It requires being real, being raw, and owning up to what is true and what we feel called by, surrendering to our organic rhythm;

It requires honesty with ourselves and with others, and a sincere choice to appear in relationships with great transparency, authenticity, and communication.

It requires deep curiosity and also a deep love of creation, of creating.

Of building under a vision that is greater than 'us'.

To come together with intention and purpose.

And once again, this orchestra starts within.

When I realized that finding myself 'alone' was a manifestation of the deep tensions around my sacrum, my world was rocked. I was manifesting this 'alone' in my life because there was an inside 'isolation' story, at the root of my body, which was keeping me in a perpetuating cycle of attracting systems that would reinforce that belief.

Underneath our inner limitations is always hidden a world of unification and possibilities.

Tapping into that sacral 'zone' was a love story for me. It allowed me to give birth to the first wave of the 'Sacred Womb Space' journey, a 6-month program under the movement of *'The Authentic Woman You Are'*, bringing together a group of women that were to grow in sisterhood and transparency, honoring one another in their gifts and complementarity, in their sacred power, and in their authentic voice. They were to bring awareness to and start stepping out from all the inner battles with authority, from the inner dynamics of patriarchy and from the inner competitions between the different parts of themselves. Unifying and collaborating within and out.

I was called to create this program. I was led. My sacrum was pulsating, life force was pushing, my whole body was in action without hesitation, knowing that the 'baby' was ready to come out. It was so visceral. I was in Costa Rica Pachamama Eco-Community where I had been spending regular time since 2009. It was the last day airports were open before Covid isolation, and my body told me:

'Leave. Go back to Canada and gather women to support their journey into their wombs and into who they authentically are. Into grounding in their nature, power and gifts.'

So I did.

And a new life appeared with that!

THE TRUTH AND THE JOY OF THE WOMB

Ah, the womb ...

Landing in the womb revolutionized my world in a way that never again after I was left with the uncertainty that I had access to an infinite source of energy, of love, of wisdom.

I was in a big turning point in my life then, letting go of my marriage, letting go of my yoga tribe, jumping into sharing my gifts with the world on a larger scale, starting to homeschool my son, choosing to close the door for good on my engineering career, etc. 'Where is the stable point?' That is what I was asking myself.

And my womb showed me.

When doubt arises, I drop my attention there and rest. I wait until it releases the accumulated stress and I welcome the nurturing power of its divine nectar.

When we drop into our pelvis, root on Mother Earth, and create that space around our heart, we access the natural pulsation of our organs, gaining access to infinity. We start acting out of love, from the love we are cultivating within, rather than from fear, from the fears that have accumulated in our bodies through generations and generations. We shift the shadow into light. And through this infinity and spaciousness, through the portals that open with this process, we receive inner guidance. Our organs start collaborating with one another with great joy and intimacy, they communicate and act together, in alignment with our deep desires and highest calling.

Actions become more conscious, true, meaningful, grounded and intentional. Our potential actualizes and what is transmitted from our body becomes powerful, vibrant, and touches the life of others, directly or indirectly. It inspires them to transform and embody also the most authentic version of themselves, and fiercely create the life playground that aligns with who they are and with the light they are here to bring.

My body was filled with gratitude when I accessed that new layer inside my womb. It was like everything I had been looking for was finally found. I opened myself to receive, to feel alive and to be infused by life force in a new way. I felt an immense surrender to my nature appearing then. I felt my feminine essence expand and I started making peace with it, innerstanding its natural function. I had forever operated in a more masculine way and suddenly then, something was shifting. I started feeling safe in my feminine, something I had never really tasted before.

Since then, my womb has become my compass.

It's in the seat of that amazing center that our embodied power lies, that our primal force exists, not to fight, to flee, or to survive, but to create the life we are meant to create and to live. Freer and truer.

From the womb we reset, and we encounter the ecstasy of creating and uncreating with deep felt pleasure.

Our Life becomes fierce and aligned, and we include others.

LEADING OUR LIFE IN VISION AND COLLABORATION

The image that comes to me when I tune into the gifts of collaboration is a circle, a spiral, a movement of unification and togetherness. I see joy as well as support. I see vision and direction, and I see light.

There is a reason why a group of people is brought together. Always.

There is a common longing, a common path to walk, a common breakthrough to have. This time 'together' could be for a whole lifetime, or it could only be for a year, a month or even a minute!

It doesn't matter.

Collaboration is an attitude to have as we breathe in and out, curious of the big picture of where Life is leading, of what Life is asking from us each moment. And surrendering to it.

How can I collaborate now? How can I be open?

Life is a mystery to be lived, and together we are stronger.

When everybody rises in their light and truth, all collaborations become fair. Everybody wins. Everybody grows. Everybody contributes. For me, fairness is about this: Are you in your light and truth as we are collaborating? Do you have the space to express your Godly given gifts? Do you feel safe to do so? Do you Trust?

As women, as moms, as leaders of families, communities, organizations, movements, as a spouse or as a lover, we have a direct impact on the ones surrounding us, and what we cultivate inside is either life giving or life draining for others.

Are we coming from a space of creative energy or from a space of separating energy?

When we unify and harmonize the dynamics and 'relationships' we have within, what is outside starts harmonizing and unifying too. When our body, organs, tissus, cells, are activated, when they communicate, collaborate, when they have enough space to shine their light and be received in it from within, our light starts shining, and gives back.

Then lack disappears. We vibrate more fullness and more wholeness. The parts within meet and align our lives, and we grow in collaboration.

We become creators.

We become conscious vessels.

We become embodied in this human experience, in service to the Divine.

And we Play the Game of Life.

If you would like to jump into the path presented above, take a look at the biography below and go to the link in order to receive the free *'Discovering Home Within'* 1h 30m embodiment practice. It will help you get a taste and experience directly an activation of your body through deep intimacy and connection with it. This practice is at the root of *The Authentic Woman You Are* transformation system and is designed to help you ground in your next layer of authenticity and potential, to gain clarity on your calling and to reactivate your innate power. Let me know about what you experience!

ABOUT THE AUTHOR

JENNIFER ACKAD

Embodiment and Transformation Coach, **Jennifer Ackad** left a successful Mechanical Engineering Career in 2010 to follow her soul calling. For more than 9 years, she immersed herself thoroughly into yoga therapy and other self healing schools, diving deep into her own body and self awareness to dis-cover what she now calls Home within. She has mastered the art of listening within to unleash the stuck energy, alchemize it into higher frequency and redirect it into purpose.

Jennifer's commitment to authentic living and activating one's unique potential is truly contagious. Her daily work consists of sharing the jewels that she receives on her path, giving back to thousands of people through online platforms, programs and as a featured host/guest speaker on various summits and podcasts.

Creator of *'The Authentic Woman You Are'* transformation system, she accompanies women to create space in their body and in their lives in order to awaken the wisdom, truth and answers they hold inside. Her mentoring programs are intimate containers where women gather to reignite their innate sacred power, reconnect to their intrinsic gifts and ground in their true essence. By honoring their deep desires and higher calling, women shift their lifestyle, manifesting a creative and fiercely-aligned life while empowering others.

As a homeschooling mompreneur and yogini, she chose to create her reality, spending half the year in the Costa Rican jungle as part of Pachamama Eco-Community, and the other half in the forest in Val-David village, Quebec. Her passion for Life energy combined with her devotion to growth make her a forever learner and a dedicated teacher.

To connect more with Jennifer, visit www.jenniferackad.com

To receive the Free 'Discovering Home Within' Embodiment practice video, go to https://bit.ly/AW-EmbodimentJourneyGift

Part III

COLLABORATION IN COMMUNITY

JAIME LUND

QUANTUM COLLABORATION

> "You never change things by fighting the existing reality. To change something, build a new model that makes the existing model obsolete." —Buckminster Fuller

> "No problem can be solved from the same level of consciousness that created it." —Albert Einstein

My friends call me Jai. I am here to help create a mass scale transformation of humanity into a fully empowered, conscious, thriving and cooperative species through a Change Maker Platform called Thrive Tribe Global.

We are at an incredible crossroads. Never before have our decisions or our choices as a collective been more important. People are waking up to the urgency as we see fractures and fault lines in all sectors. Many are on the verge of total collapse.

With everything going on in the world, not many would argue that we are at an intersecting existential meta-crisis. One gets the sense the music is about to stop and we need to find a chair.

We are about to see groups of like-minded people all over the world unite and create alternatives. Never underestimate what a determined group of people with similar values are capable of doing —especially when you activate their survival instinct!

How do we not only survive, but thrive at such a tumultuous tipping point in time?

I propose that behind all of this duality and divide is a singularity. One force that is guiding this transition in this great awakening. This is the energy and source that we need to draw from now and always.

I'm thankful this life has given me the great blessing of tremendous adversity, having had two near-death experiences that rendered me without a heartbeat for many minutes. I was blessed with these experiences that have helped to anchor me in the technology, systems, innovations and infrastructure of our new earth reality. I can see how all of my life has prepared me for this moment. So many of us have been prepared so we could hear the call, and then answer it when the time came. We were born for this time.

After facing death and understanding that I am not a human being having a spiritual experience, but rather a spiritual being having a human experience, my life transformed into one of constant surrender. I don't play the world game of consumption, competition and control. I moved from playing the finite game, to playing the infinite game. It changed the way I thought about everything, the way I executed my entire life. In prayer I ask the questions and in meditation I receive the answers.

My operating system has learned how to work at high levels of vibration. Miracles occur and phenomena that would normally be impossible suddenly become possible. We enter the realm of pure potentiality. The quantum field. The place where when we change the way we look at things, the things we look at change. In this thrive-state, we are in yes-mode, saying yes to all of life and letting it course through our veins. There is nothing juicier or more incredible than feeling at one with all of life and riding the wave of creation and manifestation to create the life of our dreams.

We are not taught how to access our birthright to thrive, so we are going to help you and others to access that information and knowledge that is the lifeblood of the tribes.

The youth holds the key. I vow to witness my own children and to inspire them to come into their own. Nothing prepares you for the love that is felt when your heart is walking around outside of you. There is a seismic shift in how one sees the world. As nature has designed it, there isn't much we won't do for our children.

Parenting and the challenges of raising children in this time has pressed me to find solutions and source out others who feel the same. They are the greatest little teachers and I continue to be humbled by the wisdom that comes from their still-intact celestial connections. The greatest gift I can give them is to keep this divine line intact and not to domesticate their spirits. I am the guardian of their greatness and freedom, of their sacred connection to Source and of this planet they will inherit. I am the steward of their sovereignty and I have committed to ensuring my children and those of my tribe remain sovereign on all levels.

Those I come together with now, my brothers and sisters, my soul family, fellow lions and lionesses, we are the change we want to see in the world. This bridge is the Change Maker Platform we call Thrive Tribes. I want my children and my children's children to have a beautiful and healthy planet to inherit. Too ambitious to tackle alone, but together, anything is possible. I can make bold and audacious declarations based on this fact.

The outcome now depends on the quality of our questions as this determines the quality of our answers. I've asked the big questions, then I got out of the way. "How can I be of service? How can I uplift humanity and help others to reach their human potential? How can I serve to create a thriving planet and build a new earth for our children? How can we scale change and turn this ship around—quickly? How can I open the space to receive quantum leaps in transformation that we so badly desire and require? How can we collaborate at levels we have never worked at before?"

We are in a condensed evolutionary phase. Many refer to this time as the entry into the Golden Age. We are in a massive shift in consciousness. The weeds must be pulled for us to advance. The darkness must come to light.

When we can reframe what is happening right now through a new lens and perspective, we can become empowered by the chaos.

> "All great changes are preceded by chaos." —Mahatma Gandhi

We can't solve the problems we face with the same level of consciousness that created them.

We are the only creature as far as we know that can fantasize. From the great Napoleon Hill, "Imagination is the most marvellous, miraculous, inconceivably powerful force the world has ever known!"

Don't listen to people who tell you it can't be done! Now is the time to dream big. Now is the time to fantasize, imagine and dream into being the most incredible vision for humanity. We must surround ourselves with people who inspire us!

We never know the power and the wisdom that are available to us until it's clear we have to rely on something beyond ourselves. This is the moment that we need to recognize that we are part of something much greater, that loves us beyond all we could ever ask or imagine. We have been prepared for this moment, to celebrate that we can draw all we need from this Infinite Source.

With all our heart, soul, mind, and strength now is the time to embrace the truth. It is all inclusive, and I believe transcends all religions. Be empowered to stand up and be a beacon of light to people around you, your voice, story, and strength have the power to inspire the positive change the world needs.

No one person has all the solutions. If we want to get where we need to go we need to rely on everyone working together. We must give away the power and make sure everyone feels their voice matters. We must seek to get the best out of everyone.

Quantum Collaboration is synonymous with Thrive Tribe Global. We are knitting together family, a rooting and re-stitching of the fabric of our tribal bonds. So we can look after ourselves and each other including the needy and most underprivileged of the people within our community. As individuals and members of our tribe we must decide what it is we really want.

Everything that we've created was first created in our minds and then it got manifested in our world. This is The Source of Creation. This is the heart of the tribes.

Tribes allow us to evolve into unity. Neo-tribalism, also known as modern tribalism, is a sociological concept that human beings have evolved to live in tribal society, as opposed to mass society, and will naturally form social networks constituting new tribes. We are One Tribe at the same time that we are multiple tribes allowing us to zero in and focus on individual strengths. We have to expand ourselves beyond the tribes to a global perspective.

In flux between tribalism and global perspectives, we can connect and collaborate at never-before-seen levels. It's super hard, it's really fragile, it's never been done and conditions are getting tighter.

The best way to achieve this is in small groups or tribes, part of a larger collective with a unifying goal and vision. This is called global tribalism. It's paradoxical, but aptly describes what it is to belong and to be part of a group, but to also be ONE. It allows us to work together by commonality or region to be more efficient and focused in our solutions and to implement them more quickly. It likewise breeds amplification and acceleration as tribes connect with the larger global vision, working off of precedent and standing on the shoulders of giants. The cross pollination between the tribes creates dynamic networks that allow people to join us at one entry point, only to realize there is a vast universe within which they can thrive and diversify. Awareness of the problems we face, and access to shared solutions is created as we pool resources and acquired knowledge. Growth is exponential. All members of the tribe are nourished and fed in a symbiotic and synergistic eco-system. Thriving is inherent.

We must work together, to heal the divide and remember the big picture and our common goal as humanity.

As we work towards something together we feel alive, purposeful. Instead of sitting in rows and columns, we return to the round table. We return to the Council where all members have the opportunity to speak, not as a hierarchy but as a family, where everyone can claim space and have a voice. Possibility expands exponentially. We work together in ways we never have before. In setting ourselves to really accomplish something, we have to be inspired!

The pattern, the map has been given to us. Now we need to work together to fill it in, live into it. We already have the framework to build the New Earth. We have the technology and everything that we need to achieve our goal.

Thrive Tribe Global (TTG) is based on the 12 Core Sectors of Human Endeavour; we call them tribes. They are all interconnected. Using the Thrive Solutions* model we identify problems in each of these key sectors and come up with the best ways to tackle them. We move from awareness and knowledge of the issues, dangers and problems we face, to the solutions. The dynamic nature of the tribes allows us to receive solutions from multiple perspectives and viewpoints and is therefore highly effective. It is a hotbed of cross pollination of the ideas, tech, resources, people, platforms and projects that transform our world. It is achieved both at the macro and micro level. Elevating, inspiring and igniting change is the thread that weaves all the tribes together.

It all exists but most of the truly effective solutions have been suppressed and censored. Scientists, inventors and creators have been marginalized and discredited for things like free energy and cures for cancer. Their livelihoods destroyed and lives threatened. The push to keep feeding the machine of greed, power and money has overtaken our planet. Thankfully we are at a time of convergence, a choice point, an inflection point. The current global events have turned the heat up to the point where now we are called to act, to shift, to wake up, to become aware of the sinister force that has captured our planet and overtaken a way of life that supports us sustainably. Our society has been set up to be fragmented, isolated, alienated and alone. Social distancing has amplified this 10X.

Our cosmic positioning systems have been completely hijacked. Misaligned to all the things that give us our true power. We are literally being poisoned, from the media cartel to the food that we eat, to the substances placed in our teeth, to the frequencies in music that are harmful to health and the EMFs that come from the toxic soup of radiation. We have been kidnapped from our greatness and are being held ransom by those that desire to control us. Until now, we have let them create followers, humans pliable to a mundane existence, where without question, they accept their factory fate or the need to work 9-5 or 2-3 jobs just to stay afloat. A debt system has been plotted, planned and executed for a very long time that keeps us on the hamster wheel and in survival mode.

When we are in survival, we are not thinking about how we can change the world. We are just trying to figure out how to put food on the table and keep a roof over our heads. When we are constantly trying to recover from trauma and living in our pain bodies, the conversation around thriving becomes mute. It remains inaccessible. It remains a luxury. But it is not a luxury! It is our birthright. Most of society is designed to weaken us, like kryptonite to Earthly superheroes.

We are now at a place where we must guard the embers of all living life. We have the responsibility that comes with understanding we are in a time that requires radical surrendered service to the greater good of humankind. Now is the time to bring our talents, education, specialties, pain, passion and experience to the table. We must live in the deep now to see where we have gone off-course from our alignment with Source and this disconnection we have with each other and our home, planet Earth. Now is the time to organize so we can meet the challenges we face head on with confidence and courage.

> "Those who love peace must learn to organize as effectively as those who love war." — Martin Luther King Jr.

This can be a period of fear and panic or it can be a time of spiritual transformation. Things are not getting worse, things are getting real. We must hold each other tight and continue to pull back the veil. I believe goodness will emerge again based on what we do now. I believe deep in our bones we know that we have already ONE.

The list of topics that require our attention are exhaustive. We have run out of imaginary money. The bubble is about to burst. We have to make transitions on energy sources, unravelling and unwinding old ways of being and doing things. We see a massive increase in intense weather events, we face potential impact on food supplies, increasing tightness around natural resources, namely water. We consume enormous amounts of toxic material with virtually no regard from the masses to change our habits or curb our ways of life. We are cycling through natural resources as if they are limitless. However, we know they are certainly finite. Our current sense of the crisis we are in is filled with grief, rage, despair, rape and pillage without regard to cost, environmentally or otherwise to take and keep taking and consuming; We have pushed the limits of our Earthly capacities to extremes.

We have reports saying we have 10 years to figure this out. The really smart people say we are right there, at a precarious tipping point. Mass global awakening is required to set the course straight. It's not just one thing, the bees, the calving icebergs the size of cities plummeting into the ocean, the polar bears, the waterways, the endless fighting...but the convergence of it all happening at once. We are not only faced with the elimination of species and of flora and fauna, but we are faced with elimination of the human species and life as we know it. We are on the cusp of the next great mass extinction.

There is no one coming to rescue us; we must rescue ourselves. We are the ones who will build the new Earth. As overwhelming and scary as it currently seems, we are also on the precipice of incredible opportunity and transformation.

We must accept that we are tribal social primates and we need connection. In hard times, we must come together more, not less. We must accept that we are one species and we are in this together. All the things that divide us only serve to keep us in fear and survival. We are incapable of feeling both love and fear at the same time. Now we hold space for awakened humanity to join us, we move to decentralize away from hierarchical structures that aim to control, dominate and centralize power, into the new systems that redistribute energy and resources. To create collaboration rather than competition, cooperation instead of greed, inclusiveness rather than division. The build will come through the people that are willing to be vessels for change, willing to put their egos aside to receive the intelligence that is planting the knowledge in our consciousness if we are clear, receptive and quiet. People living in collective co-creation, community, connection, cooperation, compassion, coherence, and collaboration at the highest levels.

We are calling all visionaries, lovers, artists, freedom fighters and truth igniters, healers, conscious entrepreneurs, change makers, luminaries and solutionaries to a quantum leap in collaboration who want to make an impact and change the world. We see contribution from both a regional and global level. We think globally, and act locally. On ThriveTribeHub.com we have our 12 Core Tribes, and their sub tribes, as well as a directory of our Thrive Hubs across the globe that include our Thrive Sanctuaries, our developing Cooperative Eco-Villages that span the globe. We work with blockchain solutions to create land share opportunities for our tribe members. Each Sanctuary offers WorkAway possibilities and education in permaculture, sustainable building practices, and food security.

Our education sector is called Thrive Tribe Global Academy. As we expand, TTGA will include strategic partnerships and offerings from the best teachers on the planet. In many cases, this is retro-futuristic as we marry, fuse and alchemize ways of living that we know are time tested and proven to the newest ways of living that advance our consciousness, health and human expression.

We use blockchain technology to decentralize and create solutions that allow us to scale change in a way we never have been able to do until now. Blockchain is known as a truth machine. This technology allows us to create a glorious, highly functional, highly effective and advanced Change Maker platform that organizes us globally so we can act locally.

It is a tremendous tool that can exponentially propel change. At a time when we need to move away from the centralization of power and money in the hands of the few, blockchain allows us to decentralize and activate our freedom and sovereignty in all sectors, while redistributing wealth back into the hands of the people.

Each tribe offers its own unique gift, awakening, and illumination as we become steeped in the knowledge, community and growth that each inspires.

Everything is energy. Everything vibrates. So of course, each tribe has its own frequency and vibration. Each tribe has its own geometric shape, music and color. The 7 core tribes align with the chakra system.

For example, in Freedom Tribe, we expect a very different frequency from Soul Tribe. In Freedom Tribe, we often see freedom fighters. Thrivers compelled to be on the proverbial battlefield. They typically prefer to be in action, actively fighting for what they believe in. They "take a stand" and anchor their swords to knowledge as power. They aren't always in the fight for freedom, many are simply freedom lovers, expressing a love for freedom that is based in sovereignty from the spiritual level or a deep level of alignment and empowerment.

On the other hand, in Soul Tribe, we see the desire to create change from the level of consciousness. They have no desire to be on the battlefield or to "fight". They typically align with the greatest change being created through an elevation in consciousness, a shift in frequency and vibration from the quantum level, from the unified field.

Truth Tribe is extremely active as many people are compelled to explore the truth and to find out what is really happening on this planet. It's a tribe full of a lot of questions and emotions as certain truths are illuminated and revealed.

Typically once someone feels tapped out on truth, they want to take that knowledge and put it into action. We hit a point where we don't need to know anymore before we want to do something about it. From Truth Tribe the natural progression is to Freedom Tribe where the solutions are presented and discussed. For example, solutions around our sovereignty as it relates to common law.

Boss Tribe is where our conscious entrepreneurs hang out and strategize with business how to change the world. They are at the heart of the engine that drives our movement. BossBabes is for our women entrepreneurs who deeply resonate with women in business who want to impact and inspire transformation in this way.

Wealth Tribe is a sister tribe to Boss Tribe and is also one of the drivers of our tribal economy. This is where the Quan comes from that allows us to build resources both monetarily and in the form of hard and soft assets. Good examples of this are our Shillit.Baby token vetting platform created by our Crypto Tribe to support crypto enthusiasts or newbies coming into the space and our ThrivEvolution.io Change Maker Blockchain Project.

This is currently in development as a project incubator for changemakers and Thrivers out there that have businesses, projects or charities they want to launch or scale. It's like the Fiverr of the blockchain. This is where we get to put all our love into the initiatives that say yes to life and are designed to sustain and support our planet.

Mind Tribe is a sub-tribe of Soul Tribe and Health Tribe where we deep dive into the power of the mind and our ability to create our own reality. Our Mind-Tribers are always on us about our mindsets! They keep us flying straight. Think Joe Dispenza, Bruce Lipton and Greg Braden. This is where we remember how powerful we are and that our capacity is far greater than we currently remember. We work to access more of our brain capacity and human potential. Meditation is at the heart of this tribe.

HealthTribe is all about health. Keeping our immune systems high, unlocking states of well being previously inaccessible for many. Health is our wealth and we count on HealthTribers to keep us updated on the best ways we can achieve quantum health and thrive.

LoveTribe is the helm of relationship with self, other and the Divine. It is our relationship with life itself. This tribe teaches us how to live in the heart and be more fully whole, healed and expressive to create change at this level of relationship. TantraTribe is an incredible SubTribe to LoveTribe that offers a deeper experience of the esoteric practices behind Love Relationship, both in its shadow and light aspects. Integration of both of these aspects is key.

EcoTribe is where we get to the business of caring for this incredible planet we call home. All things environmental live here, from holistic living systems, sustainable practices, climate solutions, energy alternatives, permaculture, eco-building and New Earth innovations. Earth lovers unite to collaborate and bring us the best ideas and then action it through our Thrive Sanctuaries Globally.

Freedom Families is a large tribe that houses our TTG Families. This is a very powerful tribe because within it are housed all the 12 tribes as they pertain to families and how we must navigate the world with children. Education, specifically homeschooling and schooling alternatives are big topics in this tribe and currently the need to create an income is at the forefront. This is a beautiful place of connection with other families focused on solutions.

Through the tribes we can dive into breathwork, meditation, cold therapy, sacred substance use, heal our nervous systems, digest grief, and after all the pain and suffering, healing is essential.

As we heal ourselves, we heal each other, it's who we are. This is how we as humans bless each other.

All the vibrant colours of the tribes together make white light. The One Tribe. We make a single harmony of divine oneness. Thrive Tribe Global is the expression of the spectrum. Full spectrum collaboration asks of us to take the journey into wholeness, into healing.

There is nothing that is not collaborative. Life is in constant collaboration with us. Collaboration is our natural state.

Collaboration is a living prayer.

According to quantum physics a particle vibrating due to your sound when you speak can affect a molecule inside a star at the edge of the universe instantly. This is known as quantum entanglement. The greatest illusion in this universe is the illusion of separation.

Own your beauty, intelligence and energy. Be fierce and unapologetic always. We are one race. The human race.

It is an honour to be here with you all.

The ones who think they can change the world are the ones that do.

Jaime Lynn Lund

Founder of Thrive Tribe Global and Host of ThriveTribe TV

https://linktr.ee/ThriveTribesGlobal

*Thrive Solutions Model — www.thriveon.com

ABOUT THE AUTHOR

JAMIE LUND

Jaime Lund is an entrepreneur, new thought leader, community builder & broadcaster of the ideas, innovations, businesses and people that build the new systems & frameworks for the future of freedom.

She is a filmmaker, author & speaker in the field of human potential. She is a master at galvanizing and inspiring the movements and momentum required to create a quantum leap for humanity.

She is founder of ThriveTribe global ChangeMaker platform and host at ThriveTribe Live. Jai, as her friends call her, is a leader in the DeFi revolution. She is co-founder of ThrivEvolution.io, a revolutionary DeFi projects incubator & ShillIt.Baby professional cryptocurrency vetting platform. Jaime is co-founder of ThriveTribeHub.com, a decentralized social media platform.

She is here to lead and co-create with other change-makers and to work with the New Earth engineers, architects and educators at this great time of awakening. She stands for the empowerment, evolution & upliftment of humanity. Her intention is to build a soul-aligned tribe who want to change the world.

Use her linktree to join the ThrivEvolution #findyourthrivetribe
https://linktr.ee/ThriveTribeGlobal

JASON FISHER

THE EAGLE HAS LANDED

There is a myth that eagles can live to 100 years of age, but at about 40years old and halfway through their life their talons(claws), and beaks, grow so long they can no longer catch or eat their prey, so they need to pull them out to allow re-growth and then they can eat again and double their life span. If they don't face the changes needed and go through the very painful experience of transformation by pulling out and allowing re-growth of their most important tools for survival, they will die.

There is debate as to whether this story is true or myth, but it is a very interesting opportunity to study, observe, and learn from, and has been a story that I can relate to in my own life.

The eagle is a very important animal to me. Ever since I was a child I was amazed and captivated by this awesome creature. I've always been mesmerised by their regal and elegant flight and their ability to soar and flow as one with the sky, expressing life's majesty. They represent peace to me. I'm inspired by the calm and precision they command. I am humbled, silenced, and in awe when I feel their presence.

I have had many inspirational moments with this sacred bird of prey. As a child I remember observing large Wedge Tails when on trips to the Australian desert with family, where they would glide and play and just be a presence free and wild. In North America at 21 I had an experience where a large Bald Eagle swooped and then circled me when I was on top of a mountain, and it was so close our eyes made contact and I could feel it penetrating into my being with its steely, but agile glare. We were at one. Also an incredible experience happened in Nagasaki in Japan when I was visiting a sacred site where many Catholic Priests were crucified. I had been searching for a particular spot where I wanted to pay my respects and I swear an eagle showed me the way and communicated with me, it peered into my eyes and heart, and it shared a wisdom of the land and space I was visiting, and then it thanked me for my visit and flew off. Eagles are way showers and have given me hope, and represented freedom in my life.

When I was 25, and half my life ago, I became a Long Haul Flight Attendant for Qantas, the Australian Airline. I received Eagle wings to wear on my uniform upon completion of my training, and with that symbol I joined a family of fliers and began a journey of healing and transformation that I didn't expect or plan for. My life took on the embodiment of the eagle spirit from that time. I consider it my duty to pass on my vision and share insights and freedom, and be a wayshower now where I can. As I find my way forward in my present life and learn to serve in a new way, I need to lean into the years flying and the spirit of the eagle to guide my way.

SHARING THE LESSONS OF FLYING

Flying was not just a job, but a lifestyle. I landed in a situation that was an apprenticeship to living a life of purpose, fulfilment and accomplishment. The Cabin Crew part of the company was a unique conglomeration of caregivers. My peers were a combination of individuals from all walks of life. Within the ranks there were tradies, lawyers, ex military, doctors and nurses, ex police, teachers, hospitality workers, artists, musicians etc. We were made up of mixed nationalities and international cultures from all different age groups, with openness to sexual preferences and choice. We met in an environment of care for each other and for our passengers. There was a strict code of non judgement, and acceptance of individuals as they are. We were appreciated and honoured for our uniqueness. It was a corporate, but family-like environment that taught me about our humanity. Flying taught the celebration that we simply must accept and Love each other as we are, and allow and encourage this joy.

Being a Flight Attendant was a dream career. When I first joined it was highly esteemed with 5000 applications for 50 positions being the ratio of people applying for this position. There was a magic that attracted people to the job. The environment welcomed service oriented characters from all walks of life. We were responsible for the safety and service on board. The Cabin Crew are the first responders; the firemen, ambulance, police; we're there to serve as the chef, barman, waiter, and the concierge; and we are the entertainer; and hold space as the psychotherapist, coach, healer and confidant. A Flight Attendant's role is a very, 'all rounder position', serving everyday life, just in the air. We are openly caring and compassionate, but behind the scenes we were trained to evacuate full aircraft when under pressure in an emergency and save people's lives.

Our aircraft flew Long Haul around the world from Sydney to London, Paris, Rome, New York, Japan and Asia, South America and Africa, and all through my homeland Australia. We had to be on call at all hours of the night and day through all time zones with a genuine smile on our face. We had to care, consider, and manage people with all of their baggage and their humanity. We weren't just carrying people, we were carrying souls. This stretched the role from the mundane, to the spiritual.

Collaboration was an essential part of the everyday experience on board working, or in foreign ports when resting. It was a busy and intense position where we needed to bond with purpose to accomplish our work on the aircraft, and we were like family caring and sharing, and relating when on ground. There was a high degree of positive pride and respect amongst our group.

Working in the team environment created support and also empowered the will to keep going when it could very easily give up. Often flights would be in time zones upside down to home and we just had to keep going no matter what the conditions. A team can accomplish more than the sum of individual parts and crew always get through by encouraging each other.

The crew embodied very special values and virtues that were lived daily. Joining together was essential and built professionalism and morale. A culture of positive discipline was energised with the corporate structure and the backbone of a business on purpose, but an open heartedness was expressed by the service and care role. On board crew consistently relate with others, sharpening their tools of knowing self and boundaries. Understanding other crew and passengers needs, by healthy communication and through empathy, and by reading situations quickly, was essential. It taught me about awareness and skills of observation. I learnt to listen and think before acting as much as possible. I learnt all people are basically the same. It taught me compassion.

There are challenges that are confronting when collaborating as part of a crew/team. Sometimes personalities clash or people have differences of opinion. On the plane tiredness and jet lag would test us all and keeping calm and patient with other crew and passengers was sometimes difficult. Another example is between divisions where communication could be tough due to work styles. Sometimes cabin crew who tend to be focused on service, and pilots who are more technical when on board would differ in communication and misunderstandings did occur.There needs to be systems in place to manage people and their personalities and roles, and there needs to be a way to ensure all parts of the team are included, acknowledged, supported, valued and encouraged. Structure and organisation is vital to a collective creative venture.

Cabin crew are very courageous. On board crew are there to protect life. Safety procedures made some choices very important, with survival dependent on it. For example passengers touching or playing with doors/exits in flight, or people smoking in the toilets is more dangerous than people know. Since 9/11 crew are now licenced and have authority in some cases to, "protect life at all cost." Every six months safety compliance tests have to be passed to keep licences, and this added to comradery. Sharing this expert knowledge with colleagues created a respectful relationship on board. Trusting your peers is priceless. It creates belonging and builds security.

There were super special flights like carrying our National Olympic Team and extremely challenging flights where there was death on board. Being in the air provided experience to know life, "as it is", by coming to understand some natural laws like, "things aren't always perfect", and that, "we are not always in control", and, "the only constant is change".

Crew often manage various less savoury situations. For example, some messy business on the plane we had to deal with was projectile vomiting. Somehow on aircraft it's a phenomenon that happens, despite a sick bag readily available in each seat back, passengers often are sick over other people. Travellers with smelly feet or toxic bad odour often made it tough as well. Violent passengers occasionally needed to be restrained. Often diversions due to weather, mechanical issues, or ill health of passengers, etc. redirected our flight path. Conditions were always different and every flight was special. I experienced an abundance of joy travelling, sharing adventure with passengers and crew, living a dream, and also had to deal with everyday pressures. Flying was a microcosm environment to study humanity.

The aircraft was my living room and having many visitors move through the space gave me insight to different cultures, different lifestyles, and various ways of being, and it gave perspective and refined what is important to me. It taught the true meaning of service. True service is a practice, it is a karma yoga, and is an opportunity to understand our natural being. It is a path to liberation and peace. The joy of giving was repeated constantly and I learnt how this giving is magnified, and also the moments when it was difficult to be authentic and caring was mirrored back as well. Travelling the globe again and again taught the basics of how to live a positive life experience, but it wasn't always easy, and some tough lessons came across the path. Life reflects back to you, your truth. If you're happy, life seems happy, if you're grumpy so is the world. As there was no escaping on board, the ego often got challenged.

Once on a Long Haul flight from Singapore to Frankfurt I recall a service where I had to own my shadow and seriously eat humble pie. I had been flying for about 3 years at the time, and was getting comfortable with my role and I became quite full of myself. I had just woken from crew rest where we slept on long flights. I was tired and grumpy and just couldn't shake off my blurry jetlag. I had to serve and face the economy passenger cabin and I didn't want to be there. We were somewhere over Europe and the sun was rising. The fluorescent lights were on high and 350 faces were eagerly and enthusiastically awaiting their breakfast. I had pressed on giving out Economy meals and was going through the cabin offering coffee and tea. My attitude was totally self consumed and I was blaming the passengers for my bad mood. I wasn't smiling and was quite angry, but unconsciously so, and was projecting this energy.

I recall I was pushing my way through the service, "Tea, coffee, tea, coffee?"

I got to a passenger who had a blanket over his hands. I looked at him as if he was stupid for not raising his cup to meet me, and exclaimed raising the teapots in my hands to his face, "TEA, COFFEE!?"

I had been working in another section of the cabin until this moment and hadn't met these particular passengers. The man with the blanket over his hands kindly and innocently looked up at me. The passengers on either side of him looked up at me as well, and sensitively the gentleman by the window calmly and compassionately lifted the blanket off the man who I was rude to, revealing the truth of the situation. I was way out of line. The man with the blanket over him had two severely deformed hands and couldn't hold a cup even if he tried. All the passengers in that area observed this. I immediately came back into my humanity. Ashamed and embarrassed. I realised I was being unkind and self centred and I got a great lesson in humility. Life is the teacher, and that day I learnt a lot.

We are ultimately responsible for our own reality as life is served to us in each moment, having free will and choice how we respond. Living this knowledge wisely will set us free. Owning negativity is essential. Flying provided an opportunity to constantly exercise this practice.

Through 25 years of collaborating amongst a team on an international stage, and through serving humanity and learning to honour life, my mind and heart was opened to understanding a deeper rhythm of being. The Flight Attendant career provided many experiences and a possibility of depth and meaning that far exceeded the job description and serves me now in this new world.

THE DAY WHEN EVERYTHING CHANGED

I never wanted to leave flying and wished it would never end. It was a life within life. I genuinely loved my career. Like an eagle, I felt free and alive riding in that grande metal bird and embodying natural understanding from the lifestyle. I always knew I would have to prepare for life after flying, but that was always in the future. I didn't think and couldn't conceive that I may have to adjust immediately. I wasn't prepared for landing when COVID shut down the airline and the world in early 2020.

So like the eagle who has to grow new talons and learn to eat from a new beak, I have had to go into my nest to regenerate and re-grow resources, and to find a new way to live in this new world. Being at home, after years of movement all around the planet has been joyful, and excruciatingly painful. It has been a journey of re-birth to come in for landing.

I have always held a dream within me that peace and well being is our natural way and that joy is our birthright. But I have never slowed down, or been as confronted, or gone as deep as now when facing this present situation to open this up. The airline business along with much of our world as we knew it has completely disappeared, and I've had to adapt fast and learn to navigate differently. I have found without my busy and active life flying that it isn't as easy as I had dreamed to live in authentic joy and peace. Getting earthed and coming home, facing illusions and letting go of ideals, and all that's not serving, is creating an opening and new way in feeling and being on purpose, and transformation is the theme.

CHANGE IS A PROCESS THAT CAN'T BE RUSHED

When I first came in for landing I thought it was great. A holiday and some time to rest after 25 years flying felt like fun, and I needed the space to recoup. I celebrated and partied for 3 months before I realised what I was doing. I was having the time of my life escaping, but it caught up to me. My friends and family had to call me on my behaviour and I had to start looking at the shadow aspects of myself. I realised that without my busy flying life I had to face some parts of me that I'd been keeping in hiding. A dark night of the soul consumed me and it felt like there was no way out. I went into grief and a sense of loss. I realised that I had been addicted to the fast life; lots of coffee, lots of alcohol, lots of fun, and lots of flight. And the fast life addictions were covering other unresolved elements of my being. I had to dive deep and allow the nest of home to hold me as a catharsis occurred.

I have practiced and studied the healing arts parallel to flying through the years, and thought it would be easy to come home and start the business of my dreams in this field. But it hasn't been easy. I have had to observe myself in each moment without addictions and avoidance, and learnt to confront fear and illusion.There has been no way out but through, and like the eagle in the nest, I have had to commit to the transformation process. I have had to open up and learn new things. The ego has been confronted and restructured. I have had to break down to break through. It has been a challenge and continues to test. My life flying was amazing, but it wasn't fully responsible or empowered in this way. Flying masked an underlying angst. When home, life got real. I now know that each of us has to encounter this shadow world in order to become whole.

The regrowth of the beak and talons is symbolic of my return to healthy discipline and a birth into a greater more whole self. This gift of coming home from flying, to the stillness (inner and outer), has created an opportunity to go within and travel like never before.

I have a vision. I've longed to build a healing centre where people can rest, be safe, and be themselves. It has taken some pain to open up the way, and to get specific, but it's happening. I'm bringing the positive plane environment to the land where I live. Due to being at home, it is building momentum and focus. I moved onto my land 7 years ago with a shovel and a tent. I now live in a home too big for me, and I realise that to continue to grow and manifest, I need to surrender to sharing the vision with friends and community. A healing centre is about the people. At present a team has formed around me, and it's like a crew on board a plane.

There are five mature men, a feminine Goddess to keep us honest, and the kids. We bring together our gifts for the betterment of the whole. We are practicing and sharing a meditative life with yoga, gardening, music, cooking, bodywork and psychotherapy, and shamanic healing work. We have builders and dreamers living together. We intend to invite others into our group space to serve and pass forward our gifts as a business. We have all carried a similar unified dream of what's unfolding at present, and supporting each other moving forward individually. We are visionaries sharing a new way of living.

We aim to practice meditation each morning at 5am, Zazen style (just sitting), and explore the mountain postures of yoga daily. We are a tribe, and it is similar to living in a temple or monastery setting in that the crew on the land have made a decision to explore the group dynamic with specific structures and intentions in place. We have meetings, we have basic rules, and we care for each other. This collaboration of attention makes things happen. The compassion and support that a team can bring is very wholesome. Coming together is a container for transformation. I have used the support, and the meditation to heal. Collaboration with myself is now opening the way to collaborate with others. My purpose is bigger than me, and like on the aircraft when a team/group/tribe come together with the same vision, big things can happen. The impossible becomes possible. When we come together we can achieve our higher possibilities. We can rebuild the broken parts, and mend our pained hearts and lives. We can heal the planet in this way. We can transform and feel eternity.

The 4 acres of sundrenched land where I live on the Central Coast an hour north of Sydney is surrounded by forest and water, fresh air, and the fire of our spirit, and after years travelling I don't wish to be anywhere else then here right now.

I have used all of the skills from flying to empower me into this new life and way. I know I am the creator of my reality now and am taking responsibility. I am a traveller with an eagle spirit, and love movement in the outer world and within. I am into the beauty of non-attachment and soaring flow, and am creating an environment to support this awareness. Traveling and understanding the nature of journeying, is a gift I share.

Life's mystery is grande, and consciously experiencing this journey of spirit is what truly brings exhilaration and presence. The hero's journey is something we all share. I want people to be able to take time and space to uncover their truth and experience freedom for themselves. I want to live unmasked in my raw self and invite others home to this self too. I want to bring true service and the First Class experience on-board, home, in an authentic way.

Gondwana Retreat is unfolding around me with effortless flow, ease and grace, and the next chapter is opening up. It is amazing how life is giving and supporting each step of the way, as if it's being guided. Living with this team of fellow travellers who share my vision is like Camelot. There is a magic that is opening. Flying was the foundation for this new life and I am forever grateful, but I have come in for landing and adventure, at home and in heart.

I honour the eagle for inspiring me to open my visionary potential and for it's natural bravery, teaching me how to transform and re-birth. I recommend we all tune into our nature to remember who we are, and explore and heal, and become unshakably whole. Let's find our way to our highest self, and learn how to fly into our knowing and eternal self. Let's breathe with awe and live in Love and Collaboration helping each other as we discover this new way of living that is beautiful and free. Life is a gift, and let's live it to the fullest.

Contact me to connect at ActivelyZen if I can be of value in any way.

www.activelyzen.com.au

With love, Sincerely, Jason.

ABOUT THE AUTHOR

JASON FISHER

Jason Fisher is a gifted transformational life coach, bodyworker, therapist, and healer with a meditative focus and a fearless presence.

Jason integrates and embodies over thirty years of personal and professional practice in meditation and yoga, remedial massage, and core energetics psychotherapy. He has travelled the world extensively, studying different cultures and ways, and has a grounded wisdom that serves the present moment.

Jason offers unique and specialised private sessions for individuals, couples, families, or workshops/retreats for groups or corporate teams.

Jason works towards balance, unification, and empowerment of body, mind, spirit and environment. From this place, Jason encourages people to discover and follow their heart, intuition, and highest intentions. Holding space is a way of life for Jason. He practically supports others to find their own greatness, creativity, joy and love. Realness, care, peace, and fun are his gifts.

Contact Details:
Website: https://activelyzen.com.au
Facebook: https://www.facebook.com/jasonfisher.activelyzen
Email: activelyzennow@gmail.com
Phone: +61 0414734208

KELLY BOUCHER

RADICAL COLLABORATION: FLIPPING THE PARADIGM ON LEARNING

That feeling when you lean back in your chair with a cup of tea and take a moment to catch your breath in the wake of massive life change. You breathe out the past few years. With a huge sigh, you breathe out all the challenges, the frustration, the injustice, the anxieties, the overwhelm and the exhaustion. All of it exits your body in a rush of carbon dioxide and a hint of Earl Grey! You think about how weariness permeated your bones and how the shock of loss sucked out the bone marrow. You now realise that grief has incised its story by scraping you out from the inside, and your bones have been played like a flute by lady sorrow.

Yet, you realise that your body is automatically breathing in again. A deep, diaphragmatic breath that comes all the way up from your feet. And as this slow, oxygenating force travels through you, you realise you are a body-cartography. You are a magnificent, charted territory. Mapped, travelled, surfaced and deep-dived. Followed, found and revisited. Your body-ecology is (re)seeding, (re)surfacing, (re)tracing, (re)generating. You are wayfinding your new reality. You are abundant and will return to your flourishing surfaces. These body fissures will soon be filled with moss and offer new map-lines to travel. You are a wildflower meadow!

Then you realise you didn't notice that last out-breath as you're already breathing in again...in...in...in...gulping in the sweet wind of life change.

Abundance.

Excitement.

Love.

Then, you're slapped from your reverie by the ditzy digital ding-dong signalling the end of the washing machine cycle. You jolt back into your body and realise your tea's gone cold because you've been sitting there for however long breathing the entire universe in through your feet!

And so my next life-chapter unfolds. Here on Dja Dja Wurrung Country in Central Victoria, Australia. I'm on someone else's country, in a new job, a new home and gathering a new community. Some days I don't have the energy to do much more than drink my tea before it goes cold. This is a story of return. Of coming back and circling around. A story told through the lens of recuperation and recovery. You see, I'm a recovering academic. That's right, I'm recovering from spending most of my life in some form of educational institution. Kindergarten, pre-school, primary school, secondary school and university. I even became a teacher, then a university lecturer in teacher education, and I am totally indoctrinated in a system that promotes comparison and competition. A system that told me I had to strive to achieve or I wasn't good enough, and a system that, at its worst, depleted me to the point of total exhaustion.

But this is not a negative story. My story is one of transition. From the trauma of toxic academia into recovery—through deep rest and the reigniting of innate creativity and a deep curiosity for the world. This story is for those who are searching for another way of being and doing. This is a story of hope, of curiosity and of change. A place where you, dear reader, might gain some tools to 'think otherwise' and ask questions that generate radically collaborative ways of 'living well with' the world/with others[1] in glorious multiplicity and complexity.

IN THE NAME OF WHAT?

The Euro-Western education discourse is dominated by developmental psychology and developmentally appropriate practice. This is a view of education that charts children's 'progress' via standardised systems of testing and measuring 'achievement'. This is a system that breeds competition and individualism and one that views children and childhood/s as fitting neatly into universal developmental milestones. Thus, generating a culture of comparison and competition from the very beginning of a child's life. This system frames children as deficit and as always in the process of 'becoming' something else. Children are seen as empty vessels to be filled up with knowledge and skills in order to travel through progressive milestones, or 'grow up' into productive economic citizens. These specific focuses can affect parents' own sense of comparison/competition as they navigate through parenthood with questions such as 'Is my child OK?', 'Which growth percentile are they in?', 'Where are the 'best' kindergartens, schools, universities?' However, what is missed in such a standardised view is that childhoods are messy, gloriously complex and vastly different all over the world, and children's learning experiences can't be placed neatly into universal categories. Global childhoods are multiple and complex and unfold in a kaleidoscope of family configurations and sociocultural influences.

In a neo-liberal system, the perspective that views children (learners) as somewhere to deposit knowledge and skills shows no regard for children's own voices, agency or competence as active and capable citizens of the now[2] and not just as becoming future adults. Essentially, the Euro-Western education system has indoctrinated me into preparing children/students to become 'good' economic citizens which, for governments, is the ultimate return on investment. With this in mind, as a lecturer pushing back against a tide of simplification and standardisation, I became more and more disillusioned and crippled with feelings of inadequacy; having to justify my ways of doing/thinking and prove myself over and over again. It was through this struggle, I began to wonder how an exhausted population of teachers could *ever* be cared for by a system fuelling already untenable workloads with ever more requirements for admin, compliance and government policy push-down.

Justification, accountability, competition and comparison are killing us!

By removing myself from a system that has totally depleted me over the years, I now choose to cultivate connections that nourish me and help me to step into other ways of scholarship. I'm questioning how I might 'do academia otherwise' and what that might look like in all aspects of teaching, learning and research. For me, the question here is how we might flip the paradigm on learning and, as a society, invest in children (and in turn our academic/teacher selves) to fully participate in the now?

At this point, I must be clear and say that even though I reached my limit in many aspects of teaching within the academy, I also recognise wholeheartedly that being in academia has supported me and given me many opportunities for which I am deeply grateful. I hold much gratitude for all of my wonderful colleagues. Those generous and innovative thinkers who have been so supportive of me as an emerging scholar. These are the connections that have called me into collaboration in many lively and dynamic ways. Through my teaching journey, I've found a community of scholars who engage in theories and ideas of the world that continuously challenges my own thinking. Theoretical frameworks that offer *radically* different ways of viewing the world, and that turn towards multiplicity and complexity through collective critical discourse. These ways of being and doing show me how I might attend to research *otherwise*, and question what that might look like in the everyday --in classrooms, in homes, and on the streets. Focusing on grassroots learning and everyday moments of practice.

WHAT IS PEDAGOGY?

In order to flip the paradigm on learning, first we must understand the term 'pedagogy'. Here, I will offer a few definitions of pedagogy before landing in a place where a static definition becomes active, lively and in continual momentum. Pedagogy is a term used to describe the 'art' of teaching and learning. A teacher's pedagogy is their method—how they use their tools/skills in combination. Deborah Britzman, North American psychoanalyst and education professor responds to pedagogy as *'the agency that joins teaching and learning'*[3]. I describe this definition by imagining a venn diagram, where two flat circles, one of teaching and one of learning, cross over into each other. Where the circles meet is the 'coming together', the blending and becoming agentic. However, for me these definitions still lack complexity. Christina Delgardo Vintimilla, Assistant Professor of early childhood in the Faculty of Education at York University, responds to pedagogy not as a definition, but as an active dialogue *with* the world. This dialogue, or 'becoming' is an embodied practice of 'living well' (Vintimilla, 2020), and is not confined to the traditional realm of education. This notion of pedagogy is collective, collaborative and relational, in that we are called into the act of world-making in multiple and collective ways. Thinking pedagogy as living well with the world is a radical concept in the Euro Western education system, however these are not new ideas. This concept is a response to and a thinking with Indigenous relational worldviews. Indigenous relational worldviews are rich and intelligent understandings of the world informed by creation stories and complex cosmologies. First Nations perspectives are active and lively, where humans and non-humans (Country, landforms, animals, spirit, plants, minerals) are intricately connected and in relation with each other at all times. Kathryn Coff, Yorta Yorta woman and Indigeous practitioner in residence at La Trobe University, explains being in relation as where *'boundaries between humans and nature are blurred. Things are not animate or inanimate, rather everything is animate'*[4]. In other words, Indigenous relational worldviews are agentic (active, alive and thinking) and foreground knowledge that is 'learnt, experienced and revealed [and that] all entities through relationship are equal'[5]. For me, this notion conjures up macro images of galaxies blended with the micro-worlds of living cellular structures, the life force contained in a seed, or the tenacious weed that grows out of a crack in compacted earth—bursting with insistence and liveliness.

It is through these multiple perspectives and an imaginative artistic and conceptual lens, I conjure a radical re-thinking of the education system. A proposal for *unlearning* what we already know, and courageously working toward reprogramming our neurology (thinking otherwise) by taking up our citizenship in the world collectively (and in relation). In doing so, we take up our responsibility and step into *radical collaboration* (with the world). For North American philosopher and scholar Donna Haraway, radical collaboration is seen as a cultivating of responsibility (a deep thoughtfulness to/with the world) through:

> *'...the high stakes training of the mind and imagination to go visiting, to venture off the beaten path to meet unexpected, non-natal kin, and to strike up conversations, to pose and respond to interesting questions, to propose together something unanticipated, to take up the unasked-for obligations of having met.'*[6]

In response to this I ask; what are unasked-for obligations? How do we 'propose together something unanticipated' and question what these 'unasked-for obligations' might produce? How might we take up such obligations as a collective, even when these obligations leave us entangled, slightly bewildered and somewhat disoriented? What does taking responsibility look like in the systems and structures we are so deeply embedded in as a society?

DISORIENTATION

The bewildering global events we have borne witness to across 2020/2021 have been (and are) tumultuous times of heartbreak, fear and chaos. These events demand our attention and are seen by many as a deep, impactful and exhausting, yet totally necessary disruption. Perhaps here we might view the global pandemic as doing some deeper work to disorient us. Is this the reset that is a halting slap out of the consumer world's 'business as usual' mindset? Might this be the re-frame humanity has so desperately needed in order to shake us to our core, and re-calibrate our nervous systems and reset our neurology. A reset that moves us from the dominant educational discourse that has embedded in us (as products of that system) a deficit mindset of individualism and competition.

In these times of disrupted education and at home learning, where 'deficit panic' is heightened, children are seen to be 'falling behind' in their education. However, it is not the children who are in deficit, it is the system that is charging on regardless of the chaos. Children are being marched ever onward. They are being 'grown up' to become good economic citizens. Here I ask; what might the days ahead look like if we just stop for a moment? To pause long enough to authentically activate *slow education*? How do we attend deeply to slowness in our day to day? Days that rage. Days that are absurd. Days that are doing their best to disconnect us from a collective possibility of 'now-ness'. Of cultivating our collective attention and living with the world in all of its magnificent and challenging complexity.

Donna Haraway, again, asks us to 'trouble' the world. To stir up, to make cloudy, and to think together with these disturbing, mixed up times. When we are courageous enough to sit in the disorientation, the cloudiness,

> *'our task here is to make kin in lines of inventive connection as a practice of learning to live and die well with each other in a thick present...as mortal*

> *critters (microbes, plants, animals, humans, nonhumans) entwined in myriad unfinished configurations of places, times, matters, meanings'*[7].

To me, the 'inventive connections' here are the ideas, thinkings, noticings, theories and hypotheses in/of the world that come together (collide, entangle, fall out, knot up) when we attune to the 'unfinished configurations' that emerge in practice (teaching and living) and collective thinking. This *is* radical collaboration. The challenge here (as educators or otherwise) is for us to dwell in these places too. To let the concepts and murky ideas have you...just for a moment...before the analysis comes in. Dwell in this place beside the river of 'should do's', and 'need to know's.'

Dwell.

Pause.

Linger for a moment.

The microbes will get to work to break things down, enrich the soil and activate our thinking, and together our ideas will flourish in multiple, unexpected places.

LET THE CONCEPTS HAVE YOU! A DISRUPTION AND A CELEBRATION

My story is one of turning away. Not because I failed, but because I succeeded! By standing within my politics of refusal. By turning away from that which does not serve me, I turn towards that which does—and here's how I'm doing it!

I no longer choose to be in the paradigm of the individual 'I', to remain in a culture of striving, justification and competition. I choose not to do things alone anymore—in the silo of my career, in the frantic hustle and busy-ness. I cannot impact the world nor support learners/learning in this way, let alone my own growth. I am a big-picture thinker, an artist with a conceptual mindset, and I've deeply surrendered to living courageously in a conceptual realm. The concepts have taken me and I celebrate coming to know the world through this lens. I am a citizen of the *now* and I live with pedagogical intention every day. The old education paradigm does not serve me or my worldview. I choose to see a bigger picture where learning is not institutionalised. Rather, where it is decentralised, wholeheartedly celebrated and handed over to that which cultivates rather than depletes—in radical collaboration with the world.

Anjali Nath Upadhyay, like me, is a recovering academic, she is a fierce advocate for the reclamation of grassroots knowledges and learning. In the podcast series *For the Wild*, host Ayana Young describes Upadhyay's episode, "Radical Unlearning" as

> *'remind[ing] us that because this moment is so precarious, false starts are no longer an option and recognition is not enough. Instead, we must engage in deep unlearning. Instead of remaining reliant on an exploitative and traumatising system, we are called to feel into our creative powers, honour our responsibilities and cultivate our deepest curiosities in the name of collective liberation.'* [8]

Radical unlearning and collaboration is a pedagogical response to/with the world, a call to research as learners together in the everyday. The collective disorientation we are experiencing now is painful, difficult and traumatic, yet liberating. The way in which we're used to seeing the world is being disrupted. The world is demanding more of us now. We can no longer fall back on or rely on what we once knew, nor the practices we have always participated in. In light of these demands, how then, might we *reorientate* ourselves into a collective shape? Like a murmuration of birds—thousands of interconnected individuals travelling and moving together in unison and synchronicity. A system-in-motion, ready to be transformed in an instant. What does collaboration *do* and what does collaboration demand of us in this collective space? What questions must we ask of/with the world in order to respond with collaborative mindsets?

What if our most radical act of changemaking was, in fact, collaboration?

PERSONAL AND COLLECTIVE EXPERIENCE (INTO COLLABORATION)

My personal transformation has led me into recovery through a process of radical self-care. I trained in a healing modality that helped me to reprogram my unconscious mind, and release old trauma, negative emotions and limiting beliefs. This is a modality that works to change our neurology so we are no longer trapped in repeating stories, patterns and cycles. Through these processes, what I realised was that in order to move from the individual 'I', (the 'my needs are the most important in the world over anyone else' entitled 'I') into the collective 'we' is to heal the self first (cliched but true). When we activate authentic self-care and take radical responsibility for our own inner transformation and healing, we orient ourselves towards the collective because we get out of our own way and kick our ego-centric righteousness to the curb. This is how we reseed our neurology. Our inner ecology is nurtured into growth and our life becomes that magnificent, flourishing wildflower meadow.

My work in education now focuses on bringing together multiple modalities. I support educators (and others) to critically question their practices and philosophies in order to expand, learn, grow and impact the world. I am an independent scholar, an education consultant and a personal breakthrough coach. I help teachers and organisations across the education sector to activate collective critical dialogue in order to create dynamic and generative conditions for learning. By facilitating robust exchanges within theory and practice, I nurture research culture within education settings. This in turn helps teachers reconceptualise what teaching and learning could be. In the personal coaching space, I support individuals (teachers or otherwise) to transform their everyday lives by becoming curious life-long learners and active citizens of the now.

And the best thing is we are doing it together! In doing this work, we are a collective of change makers. Through my programs, we are co-collaborating, co-researching and journeying together to impact each other's lives and the lives of children and their families. Together we are gathering thoughts, ideas, questions and wonderings. These programs facilitate innovation and change-making in learning. They release the conditioned ways of the old world and make us whole, so we can create new world connections, and generative and holistic relationships fuelled by curiosity and wonder.

We are radical collaborators!

For an actual experience into a new world of collaboration and thinking otherwise, join me on the journey and experience my free Masterclass on Radical Collaboration https://view.flodesk.com/pages/612c4b21876c79b782e6861d where we unpack some of the questions I've posed in this chapter --a taster of how my programs support critically reflective discourse and creative thinking.

I look forward to meeting you!
Kelly

---

1. Vintimilla, C. D. (2020). What is Pedagogy? Pedagogist *Network of Ontario Magazine, 1*(1). Retrieved from https://pedagogistnetworkontario.com/what-is-pedagogy/Vintimilla, C. D. (2012). *Aporetic Openings in Living Well with Others: The teacher as a thinking subject* [unpublished doctoral dissertation]. University of British Columbia.
2. Iorio, J., Hamm, C. & Krechevsky, M. (2020). Going Out and About: Activating children as citizens of the now. Global Studies of Childhood, doi:10.1177/2043610620969195
3. Britzman, D. P. (2012). *Practice makes Practice: A critical study of learning to teach.* Suny Press. p. 54
4. Coff, K. (2021). Learning on and from Country: Teaching by incorporating Indigenous Relational worldviews. In *Indigenous Education in Australia* (pp. 190-201). Routledge. pg. 195
5. Coff, K. (2021). Learning on and from Country: Teaching by incorporating Indigenous Relational worldviews. In *Indigenous Education in Australia* (pp. 190-201). Routledge. pg.196

6. Haraway, D. J. (2016). *Staying with the Trouble: Making kin in the Chthulucene*. Duke University Press. pg. 130
7. Haraway, D. J. (2016). *Staying with the Trouble: Making kin in the Chthulucene*. Duke University Press. pg.1
8. Young, A. (Host). (2020, July 3) Anjali Nath Upadhyay, M.A.[2] on Radical Unlearning /190 [audio podcast episode]. In *For The Wild*.
   https://forthewild.world/listen/anjali-nath-upadhyay-on-radical-unlearning-190?rq=Anjali

ABOUT THE AUTHOR

KELLY BOUCHER

Kelly Boucher is an independent scholar, education consultant and personal breakthrough coach. She holds a Bachelor of Fine Arts, post graduate studies in education and is a qualified NLP, Time Line Therapy®, and hypnosis practitioner. Her current work supports teachers across the education sector by activating critical dialogue within theory and practice to 'think otherwise with the world'. Kelly presents at education conferences both nationally and internationally and her recent publications focus on place and materials as relational learning opportunities for children. In 2019 the content in her co-authored book chapter, "Engaging with Place: Foregrounding Aboriginal perspectives in early childhood education", was cited as a best practice scenario for children's learning by the *Victorian Curriculum and Assessment Authority*.

Kelly believes there needs to be more thought leaders in early childhood education. She serves early childhood organisations by providing coaching programs, masterclasses and online courses that help generate theory informed strategies to shift out of standardised practice and into pedagogical innovation.

In the personal coaching space, Kelly supports individuals (teachers or otherwise) via focused breakthrough programs to transform out of being stuck and unmotivated, and into alignment and flow.

Kelly thinks with concepts, lives slowly on Dja Dja Wurrung country and is cultivating her own inner ecology next to a huge eucalyptus tree.

Website: www.kellyboucher.com.au

VANESSA FRAZON NELSON

THE TREASURES IN OUR NEIGHBORHOOD

On a bright, warm summer afternoon in 1980, when I was perhaps two years old, my mother and father and I were taking a leisurely walk through our suburban neighborhood in Westmont, Illinois, just a bit outside of Chicago. There wasn't much traffic, and we had the benefit of a clean sidewalk to guide us past lawn after lawn of neatly mowed grass and floral details in the mulch near the houses and sometimes alongside the sidewalk.

I was an outgoing, unafraid toddler, and I had gotten a few paces ahead of my parents, who were walking hand in hand. Suddenly my mother found herself running to catch up with me because I had spotted a little girl behind the storm door of one of the homes and decided that I was going to come over for a visit. I zipped up the short sidewalk on short little legs and let myself in. By the time my mother caught up, she found herself awkwardly waiting for the homeowner to answer the door to the house because the other child and I had disappeared into the shadowy inside.

I saw automatic friendship in any person I met, boldly jumping in with both feet. More than once I introduced people I had just met to my parents as my best friend or as the boy I was going to marry when

I grew up. The individual in question would stand beside me, sometimes hand in hand, nodding happily. I was living through a lens of love. Everyone could be my ally and even my partner. I trusted people, loved cooperation and collaborative play, and I felt safe in the world.

A few years later, my little sister and I sat in the backyard and drew a completely arbitrary "treasure map". I was no older than seven, and she, no older than four. The map had a big number of steps this way and then that, and then back the other way, and we intended to take this path blindly across the backyards of our neighborhood—away from 55th street, of course, which was the busy road in front of our house—and going that direction would be dangerous! (Are all the mamas in the crowd cringing with me?) But I just knew going through the neighbors' backyards would be perfectly safe.

We started trekking out across the back yards—first, we crossed over the garden behind the Kims' house. (They babysat us sometimes, so their backyard didn't count as exploring.) Then it was a hundred steps this way, a couple of hundred steps to the right, back-up twenty steps. Turn in a circle around a tree—ok, now I'm embellishing, but we found something really cool! The neighbors about four houses into the neighborhood had a brightly painted chicken coop with 6 or 7 REAL white-feathered (and surprisingly smelly) chickens in it! For a kid growing up in suburban Chicago, that felt like finding treasure! That's about where my father caught up with us. Spankings weren't considered excessive punishment back then. I'm certain we received them, but I remember more distinctly wondering what was beyond the chicken coop. Would I discover horses next?

My mother tried to warn me that not everyone was to be trusted. I didn't fully believe her at first. Mr. Rogers had me convinced that all the people of my neighborhood were working together to create a harmonious, cooperative, safe world!

As I got older, I heard stories of stranger danger, kidnappings, and disappearances that happened in my world. The lyrics of two songs of the time haunted me - both by the Doors, whom my father listened to devotedly. *People are Strange*, which warned, "...when you're a stranger, faces look ugly when you're alone...when you're strange, faces come out of the rain..." And *Riders on the Storm*, which always spooked me with the sound of the rain falling behind the music, and the lyrics, "There's a killer on the road... let your children play. If you give this man a ride, sweet memory will die. Killer on the road." Jim Morrison probably did more to help my mother keep me 'safe' than she ever knew.

By the time I was a young adult, my free spirit and natural trust of people took over again.

My father says I would make him really nervous when I would take off for Nebraska from our home, 20 miles outside of Kansas City, Missouri, with just $10 in my pocket and an overnight bag. (Gas was cheaper - much cheaper!) It was only a 4-hour drive.

When I got married, my husband was part of the US Coast Guard, and he got deployed to St. Petersburg, FL. I was lonely there. My husband was out to sea for up to two weeks at a time, and when he was home, he was on the boat almost every day, overnight on many of them. I held three jobs at once to fill my time and be around people, but I didn't really connect deeply with anyone there. I didn't know how to develop relationships as a lonely married woman in an area where everyone I knew either wanted to go to the clubs or just stay home with their children.

My husband and I decided to have a baby, thinking it would take at least several months to be successful in conceiving because of timing and the relative unpredictability of conception success among our peers. Nope, I wasn't off of birth control for two months before we conceived. Luckily, I had already kicked caffeine and had started taking supplements to help any pregnancy that could happen to be a healthy one. These were suggestions I had found in the parenting books that I had been reading as early as in high school so that I could be super-prepared for my children to arrive when I was ready to welcome them into the world. (Retrospectively, I studied babyhood and toddlerhood, but I assumed I knew how to handle the rest of the years pretty well. I probably should have studied more.) But there were still some big questions ahead of me. Searching the questions that were most perplexing to me took me to a website called breastfeeding.com—and if you go searching for it now, it's very different than it used to be.

It was a board of experienced mothers all collaborating to answer pressing questions and concerns from other mothers. And even better, many of the mothers on the boards were nurses, doulas, and lactation consultants. I was so grateful to have found such a wealth of information and nearly instant answers for any questions I had about my pregnancy and beyond. And what's funny is that I wouldn't even really comprehend the full value of these connections for years.

The questions presented and answered there varied greatly. Whatever you had to ask, there was always someone who had a resource to help out. Sometimes someone would post a photo, asking, "please diagnose this rash," and ten, twenty, fifty mothers would chime in with things like, "looks like thrush, I had it and fixed it this way..." "Here are some articles with pictures that look like what you're showing us," and "I don't know what it is, but I'm following this thread because my kid has something similar."

Someone else might post, "My baby won't sleep through the night; what do I do?" Answers would pour in.

The unexpected benefit of being part of a collaborative help board like that was that whatever we learned by helping one mother overcome her particular puzzle, we now knew for when our own children had similar needs.

More than one tongue-tie was identified on the boards. More than one supply issue was solved. More than one allergic reaction was identified and remedied. Multiple moms were encouraged and empowered that they were enough and supported to advocate for their children. Multiple families were savvier to safe car seat installation because of that board. Many babies who would have struggled had the opportunity to thrive because of the community we built. These numbers are super-conservative because at least one of these items was front and center every single day on the boards.

We shared so much real-life—conception, birth, loss, illness, milestones, divorce, remarriage, stepkids, and interestingly enough, some debates, too.

You can't have a group of over 100 women from all of the US and the rest of the world and have everyone agree on all things.

We had a specific board for that—the aptly named 'debate board'. If people disagreed on a matter and it started to get heated, we'd ask them to take it to the debate board because the other boards were for support. And we took a lot to the debate board—politics, popular opinion, unpopular opinion, discipline matters, weaning ages, vaccines, and more. It was a place you could go and get thoroughly flamed. Like trigger the crap out of you FLAMED! You had to have thick skin to be there—or develop it quickly, but it was where the action was—and curiously enough—it was where the real relationships were being forged because there was true authenticity there.

15, 20 years later, some of the longest-running friendships among the group were developed right there in the middle of the arguments among a group of mothers who cared immensely for our children and for the world and approached the hard topics together while under the hormonal influences of pregnancy, the postpartum phase, and lactation.

What was remarkable about it was the practice of compartmentalizing the topics. You could be in a heated discussion with another mom (or 10) on one thread, but on another thread, someone with a crisis would be asking for help, and the answers on that thread would be fully nurturing and helpful, and collaborative—

from those same women in the discussion on the other page. In fact, you might even tag one of your debate opponents if she had more experience with that topic. It wasn't a competition. It was the village that it took to raise those children.

Our group found one another on MySpace and then Facebook afterward. On Facebook, we've been going strong in a private group for quite a few years now. In this group, we've started to support one another through the stages of parenting teens. (It's like another toddlerhood with bigger people who have more exposure to the world!) There are so many new topics we didn't anticipate when our littles were little. Teenage drama, gender re-identification, how to guide our kids through dating, sexual maturation, going off to college, how to discipline our growing kids. There are a lot of conversations right now that center around how to respectfully set boundaries for hormonal teens. Some of us are becoming grandmothers!

Additionally, as a kind of social-media neighborhood watch, we tend to stick up for each other when one of us is targeted online. If someone gets aggressive against one of us on social media, a quick post in the group can get a literal army of moms to come to our defense so that the person being attacked doesn't have to engage in the conflict, but the attacker will be pushed back effectively. Sometimes we don't even notice the attack before the girls are offering to stand up for us.

We have rallied behind nonprofits that one another support and sent crazy amounts of donations. Members have been present for one another's court cases. We have supported individuals who had experienced child or spousal loss. We pooled resources together to pay for a therapy program for one of the kids in the group who was having suicidal ideation.

I could list many more examples of how the group has been there for members. One comes from my own recent adventures.

I moved to Oregon from Missouri this summer—in the middle of a pandemic—after a difficult custody battle that really zapped all of my mental and emotional resources. I sold everything and loaded just the most essential things (clothes, cats, computers) into my old car and hit the road to make the drive to Oregon so I could share custody with my children's father. I won't get into the details of all of that—but part of my arrangement to get out here included free lodging for a few weeks by volunteering on a farm because the farm owners were both recovering from surgeries.

On the morning I would have begun the drive that would have concluded my four-day trip, my car failed to start. I was six hours from my destination. Now, several members of the group had already sent a little bit of money my way to make sure I had my hotels covered for the trip, and I should have been fine financially at that point, but I had an unauthorized charge hit my account the night before the car issue, and it wiped out my balance.

I was stranded with no resources, but I had a commitment to help this couple out on their farm and a set arrival date. I didn't want to let them down. I was reluctant to ask my girls for more help because they had already been so generous, but I knew that part of what they would do would be to collaborate on ideas for solutions I hadn't considered. I put the question to the group and then worked to find what resources I had local to me.

Ultimately, my girls made sure I had enough money for a tow. I found a kind couple in the town I was stranded in who were willing to drive me three hours west, and one of the other moms from the group drove the other three hours to pick me up at the halfway point because she lives only 30 minutes from where I'm staying now. She even had a cheeseburger waiting for me in her car when we reached her.

I felt for me that this reinforced that my community was strong across the nation and that I wasn't alone, no matter where I am. It reinforced my sense of freedom and safety. It allowed me to move forward with necessary things without fear.

And you know what's in the pasture across the street from the farm where I'm staying? Horses!

I have the most resourceful, most amazing group of women on my side, and many of us admit that our lives are made so much better because of our community.

That kind of connection and community—without competition—in complete love (I won't say there's no judgment—we're mothers, not angels.) is precisely the kind of energy we need to create over and over in the world today. It is loving, supportive, and healing.

I have seen collaborative circles develop and thrive in a few different arenas of my world—like the Next Generation Unity group I belonged to at Unity of North Atlanta. We had a reputation in the church for volunteering for almost anything. We ran our own fundraisers and gave back to the community, eagerly helping with other ministries when asked. We collaborated with other ministries to make things happen like garden projects, hosting homeless families, set up for events like World Day of Prayer, a Holistic Fair, and a fun, family-centered festival called Super Happy Fun Day. We even put on a Laser Rave in the church. We could frequently get people working together to serve the community at large.

In another circle, I have a lovely, collaborative group developing as well. I have relationships with several other book publishers. Like Krystal Hille, the publisher of this book. We all share our talents and expertise with one another to help each other develop our companies into whatever feels most aligned for each publisher. Some like to do solo-books, some want to do podcasts, and we all support anyone in our group with their ambitions. It is a group of women being made stronger not by what we compete in—but by what we share and collaborate on.

The days of people fighting each other to get ahead are gone from the circles that I keep. I have stepped away from any energies that feel that way, and I keep attracting more collaborative opportunities that are healing the wounds of competition and rivalry that others before us faced. Even right now, in this co-parenting relationship with my ex-husband, my moving to Oregon is supposed to ease opportunities and support efforts for collaborative parenting through our kids' teen years.

One of the things that we are coming to more collectively accept as a society is that we are all one. What we do for another, we also do for ourselves. Perhaps not intentionally, but we benefit by supporting what benefits others.

This shows up in at least one of the modalities that I use to serve my clients and help them practice emotional hygiene so that they can let go of unnecessary influences on their sovereignty.

When we are upset by something someone has said or done or something that has happened within our scope of awareness, we are giving those things agency in our lives. We are under its influence. This can happen with other people, events, news, memories, or even made-up scenarios we're playing to keep upsetting ourselves over and over. We may be harboring feelings of indignance, fear, anger, defiance, sadness, rage, shame, embarrassment, and so much more! These kinds of energies can easily but unnecessarily get in the way of collaborative efforts. You don't have to have these kinds of emotional reactions to much of anything, really—and they certainly don't need to linger more than the moment it takes to remind you that what has happened is not in alignment with what you aim to create in your world. You have the ability to neutralize their effect on your experience.

My favorite method to use to free people from the shackles of unwelcome thoughts and feelings is Emotional Freedom Technique (EFT Tapping). It's profound and powerful when used to clear negative thoughts and emotions—especially with the guidance of a trained and experienced facilitator like myself. But it has an interestingly magical extra bonus when used in a group setting. When multiple people are tapping along with the practitioner and the client, many of those people will see an improvement in their own emotional wellness too! This is called "Borrowing Benefits".

So, let's imagine that I'm tapping with my client, Ms. A, about her fears of success and failure. Let us also imagine that we are being observed by Mr. B and Mrs. C, who are tapping along with us while they observe. Then not only will Ms. A have a significant reduction of fear and increase in empowerment, but Mr. B & Mrs. C can both expect that their own concerns about success and failure will be measurably improved by having tapped along with Ms. A's session. All 3 may also see improvements in their procrastination, anxiety, and focus since these would be related items.

This phenomenon, unique to EFT tapping, was first recognized by Dr. Jack Rowe, Ph.D. It was later corroborated in multiple other studies.

This means that we can use EFT tapping to aid multiple individuals in releasing similar emotional blocks simultaneously. EFT tapping has been used successfully on nearly everything, including allergies and PTSD. I have personally helped clients overcome addictive eating habits, grief, and broken hearts, guilt, anger, procrastination, indecision, self-worth issues, professional obstacles, physical pain, phobias, homesickness, night terrors, and so much more. Imagine the benefits of reaching multiple people to address these kinds of emotional issues in the time it normally takes to help just one!

This is why I offer tapping circles for those who don't want to invest in a private EFT package with me yet. It may not be as intense as a focused session, but it can certainly improve your emotional hygiene so that you don't have inappropriate emotional moments when it's not the time or place for that. And so others can't manipulate you by pushing your buttons! When you deactivate the buttons, they can poke all they want, and it won't phase you. You may even find it amusing to realize how unbothered you are by things that used to be hot-button issues.

This is a confirmation that we are designed to support one another's healing and to benefit from participating in healing each other. This is a time for us all to be coming together to co-create better futures, collaborate on bigger goals, and to let go of the competition-based models of the past.

We're making the map up as we go—but who knows what kinds of treasures we'll find in our neighborhood!

ABOUT THE AUTHOR

VANESSA FRAZON NELSON

Vanessa Frazon Nelson is a Publisher, Editor, Manifestation & Goal Coach, as well as Emotional Freedom Facilitator (EFT). Vanessa received her EFT Training through EFT Universe and has been practicing for almost 10 years. She also has a BA in Creative Writing.

Her mission is to help people reach their own desired type of freedom through the strengths hidden in their shadows and the dreams in their souls. She empowers her clients to experience improved relationships, lessened pain, greater vitality, and new-found clarity, purpose and courage.

She also guides those who are called to create compelling, bestselling books to inspire others, so that they can expand their voices, leave a meaningful legacy, and live a fully-authentic, empowered life!

Vanessa conducts powerful EFT group tappings and manifesting events full of collaborative support and borrowed benefits (where the observers of a healing opportunity also receive measurable results from participating in a target's healing).

If you'd like to participate in an upcoming EFT circle, or if you'd like to discuss the possibility of deactivating some hot-buttons for yourself, please visit EmpoweredFreedomNow.com to find an event that speaks to your wishes.

*For a limited time, readers of this book are invited to attend 1 EFT circle for free ($100 value).

Vanessa Lives near Salem, Oregon with her 2 children and 2 cats. Pieces of her heart are forever in Kansas City and Atlanta.

PART IV

COLLABORATION IN BUSINESS

ADRIANA MONIQUE ALVAREZ

ALONE WE GO FAST, TOGETHER WE GO FAR

Being American is synonymous with being competitive. Winning is everything in this culture and most people will do anything to come in first. I was no different. I was always striving for straight As and to be the best. But after finishing high school, the thought of continuing this game into college bored me. The problem was I was the kid everyone expected to go to college and climb the corporate ladder. I never did either. I followed my heart and life-long dream of traveling the world and this is how I learned how to be interdependent.

At twenty years old I unpacked my duffle bag at the state-run orphanage in Tirana, Albania. The two biggest things I learned as a solo traveling volunteer were: to trust my instincts, and if I wanted to accomplish anything to do it with the help of another.

As we navigate the unique challenges and opportunities of this season our generation has the chance to see through why competition has been sold to us.

When people work together, the possibilities are endless.

When people are divided, they are doomed.

Every government seeks to divide.

Every educational institution.

Every religion.

If you look at how our society is set up, it is intentionally to create groups and classes that inherently tempt us to see ourselves as superior or inferior to another.

The sometimes subtle, other times overt message is that there is not enough, therefore we must fight it out and claim our position.

Can you think of a time in your life when you felt the need to fight for your piece of the pie?

What ultimately led me to learning and practicing collaboration was living thousands of miles away from every family member and friend. I didn't speak the language, I had no relationships, and I had to figure out how to thrive.

The very first thing I did was find someone who could be my translator and teach me Albanian. Every single thing I needed, I went to her and I asked her who she knew. Getting anything done came down to this one thing: who you know.

When I had to apply for a visa, I was accompanied by my friend's neighbor, who was an attorney. The paperwork was done over a coffee and Turkish delight.

When I got sick, I was given a shot of raki and a wedge of lemon from my friend's Grandma.

When I was looking for an apartment, it was coordinated by a friend who was a realtor and he negotiated everything for me.

What ultimately made me fall in love with Albania and continue to visit for the last twenty-plus years, was the people and all the relationships I had made.

When I returned to the U.S. after getting malaria in Africa, I returned to my home country a different person. I actually saw my culture for the first time and it was hard to swallow. Before that it was 'how it was'. I didn't know any different. I thought it was how everyone lived.

A year later I met my now-husband on a blind date on a hot summer night in Arizona, and little did I know he would become the ultimate collaboration partner. What I appreciated most about him from the very beginning was his ability to appreciate my personal freedom. He didn't have a desire to control me, my ideas, or plans. When we got married we knew only one thing: the American Dream was not our dream.

As a newlywed I told him, "I don't care if we have to live out of our car, I do not want us to give our lives to a job and boss and retire at sixty-five years old. I do not care about insurance and 401(k)s. I want to share my life with you. I want to enjoy our time together. I want us to create the life we want."

The next year we started a business together and did just that.

In 2009 most people were sure the sky was falling. The economy tanked, the stock market crashed, and the real estate market followed. Millions were losing their homes and the future felt uncertain.

I spent that same year taking someone to breakfast, lunch, and dinner. I found out why they started their business and what would help them most in that moment. I became a connector and weekly sent referrals to those in my network.

By the end of the year we had made six figures despite all the doom and gloom. It was because I leaned into relationships and helped others get what they wanted.

Most people are shocked when I tell them Derek and I have worked together, from home, for the last 12 years. Even more interesting is that we are more in love now then the day we got married. How does this work and why is it so rare?

My observation is that most married couples are actually living as roommates. Two people who are passing each other from time to time, two dreams, two visions under one roof, but rarely a team truly working together.

Derek and I came together and defined what we wanted most and worked from that place. We also looked at where our natural strengths are. We determined what each of us would be responsible for, and we made the agreement that we would stay in our lane.

Respect, rather than control, has been our guiding light.

We have never fought about business.

We have fought about many other things, like when he doesn't get to the table when the food is hot, or who forgot to put the butter in the fridge, but never about business.

Another thing my travels influenced was us having fun together. I learned overseas that people enjoy life, no matter how much or little they have. Sharing meals together, laughing, making memories are regular occurrences.

From the beginning we went on weekly date nights. I remember people laughing when I posted stories and photos online. "Dates? You're married!" Exactly! We have rarely missed our dates, even after having two babies in twelve months, and three years later losing our daughter. Our time together has always been non-negotiable.

What this has taught me is to look for a few things when I am considering collaborating with others:

1. Do we have a shared vision and desired outcome?
2. Do we know the role each of us will play?
3. Is there mutual respect?

4. Is there an agreement to mind our business and not micromanage each other?
5. Is there a strong enough of a personal relationship beyond the scope of the project?

If any of these are shaky the project will be compromised.

The number one reason for failed collaborations is a desire to control another.

This has been on my part, and sometimes on the part of the other party. Most successful people will confess to being control freaks. What is required to release this is a willingness to see that we can go much further together.

One of my favorite quotes says, "If you want to go fast, go alone; but if you want to go far, go together."

Evolving as a society hinges on this question: do we want to go alone or do we want to go together?

As our co-creation grew and strengthened I was introduced to another form of collaboration.

Five years ago while living in Guanajuato, Mexico I heard an audible voice ask me to wake up each morning and ask what was mine to share in my business. I was told it was time to collaborate with Spirit and God, to ask for guidance in everything, and to not keep how I was working a secret.

This was a season of huge growth as I often received inspired ideas for my clients, but I never told them how the ideas arrived. I was a business consultant and my fear was that people wouldn't take me seriously anymore. I faced my people-pleasing tendencies and began to let the masks fall. I was less interested in playing a role and more committed to being myself.

It turned out that many people appreciated this authentic and transparent me. Some didn't but it actually felt like a relief to lose those who couldn't love me exactly the way I am.

With each day I heard the message more clearly. The ideas were amazing and so well received. Last year while relaxing in my Grandma's recliner, I received the idea to teach women how to start publishing houses and help more voices be heard.

Many people have asked me, "Why did you start a publishing house and then create competitors?"

That isn't how I see it though.

What I could see from a higher and more expanded perspective was that many women's voices are being shut down due to endless gatekeepers and censorship in traditional publishing. I was being asked to change this, and there was no way to have a global impact on more female voices being heard if I was the only one.

It is going to take a network of female-owned publishing houses in order to exponentially shift this outdated model of publishing.

I teach my clients everything that worked for me and everything that didn't. I champion them and their success is our success. What matters to me is the big picture vision of 10,000 female-owned publishing houses by 2027.

I can only do so much, but with the help of others we can do *so much*.

One of the other ways I collaborate with my clients is I share my teams. Every person who can help them get a book edited, formatted, designed, and to bestseller status, they get an introduction to. Every service provider beyond that who could help them get on podcasts, featured in the media, and help them grow is also open to them.

I also featured several of my clients in my latest book, *How To Start A Six Figure Publishing Company*.

The bottom line is, if my clients are doing well, I am doing well.

This is how we shift the old way of thinking.

This is also how we tap into true abundance.

If the idea of collaboration feels risky here are a few things to consider in your own quiet time:

*Do I believe I live in an abundant Universe?

*Is there always more than enough for me?

*Do I feel safe?

*If others do well does it take anything away from me?

*Do I allow others to shine around me?

*Is there insecurity and fear alive in me?

*Do I feel safe around successful people?

*Is there a part of me that is afraid to shine?

*Do I own my power? And do I allow others to stand in theirs?

*Is it comfortable for me to speak my truth?

I was at a conference in Phoenix once and the man on stage said something that has stayed with me for years:

¨*Most of our problems as a society stem from a deep-seated fear of each other.*

It starts as young children the second a mother says, 'Don't talk to strangers!'

It continues as adults who never acknowledge or speak to their neighbors.

Are we afraid of each other?

Are we afraid of being taken advantage of?

Are we afraid of being hurt?¨

Most of humanity is living their lives from a place where all of this is a very real and scary possibility.

Is it no wonder we are not working together?

What if we gathered our courage and began by telling our children to speak to every person they encounter?

What if we looked each other in the eyes?

What if we thought of something kind to do each day?

What if we were generous?

What if we consciously decided to be a blessing?

What kind of world would this create?

No doubt a place where co-creation and collaboration are the norm.

May this be the world we create for our children. Let's do it together!

ABOUT THE AUTHOR

ADRIANA MONIQUE ALVAREZ

Imagine a world without gatekeepers and censorship. This is what inspired Adriana Monique Alvarez to start AMA Publishing. She teaches women how to start highly profitable publishing companies, and has written *HOW TO START A SIX FIGURE PUBLISHING COMPANY*, which is available on Amazon. She's a USA Today bestselling author and her most recent book, *THE YOUNGER SELF LETTERS* debuted #1 on bestseller lists internationally.

She has been seen in *Forbes*, *Huffington Post*, *International Living*, *America Daily Post*, *Daily Grind*, *Addicted2Success*, *Elephant Journal*, *London Daily Post*, *Entrepreneur*, FOX, ABC, and NBC.

She is currently living in 'the middle of nowhere', Colorado where she is renovating her grandparents´ home and learning how to homestead with her husband Derek, and two sons, Sam and Grant.

Website: https://adrianamoniquealvarez.com/

BRIGID HOLDER

THE THREE C'S = COMMUNITY, CONNECTION, COLLABORATION

Like most young people, I didn't really know what I wanted to do with my life. I didn't go to university; I moved to the big smoke from our small country town and became a corporate businesswoman by default.

I've been in business since age 18, and though I was pretty much just a kid, I grew and thrived in that corporate environment. I know now, it was all a part of the universal plan, at the time I felt I stumbled onto my purpose intuitively, and then worked or earnt my way into boardrooms.

The universe planned for me to be on the top side of the business world, it felt so natural to me, I enjoyed being there. Even from the reception desk in my first ever J O B, I watched and observed people in the environment. Like a nature program on TV, I could see who thrived and who struggled and why.

At the top of the food chain were the team players. They scratched backs, pitched in where they could, shared ideas with everyone and treated all colleagues as equals. Communication at the team player level was like ease and grace, they often communicated their plans and their goals were public knowledge. I learned good leaders had these traits, unlike the opposite group.

The species who worked like it was 'every man (or woman) for themselves,' who chose a lone path; this group lost sales, clients, opportunities and they were unpopular in the workplace. Their competitive nature made them seem untrustworthy, and they had trouble building relationships.

Even back then, I could clearly see the heavy weight of competitive energy holding these people back from reaching their goals.

I didn't need a university degree to learn on the job, I saw openings and learned through experience. I do have an accounting diploma, that only came about because my boss was floundering at accounting tasks. Out of my own frustration, I studied to take over those responsibilities. By taking these tasks off him, I saw it as freeing him up to do what he did best, little to nothing. That's how I landed in the role of qualified company accountant– a position I did not love but excelled in, so I kept going. The realisation that being open to opportunities could actually lead to more for me.

Initiative like mine is probably why I continued to succeed in the business world. When I saw a job that needed doing or an area where I could contribute more, I took it. Even if it meant challenging myself to learn new skills.

Time went on and I started slipping into competition against other organisations. It didn't necessarily feel right but I had not yet honed my intuition, nor did I trust it. It's the first time I experienced the dreaded imposter syndrome. That combined with some less-than-ideal advice sent me down a path of mistakes that taught me lessons that I used to change the trajectory of my life.

But first, the poor advice, and how I shut down my inner voice. Have you heard of S.W.O.T. analysis? We learned about it in one of the training sessions I attended through work. Strengths, Weaknesses, Opportunities and Threats. The presenter told all participants to "go ahead and pop the names of any organisation that does the same or similar as yours does in the 'threats' section'. There I was again, back in the jungle, predators and prey. Naturally, I questioned the logic.

I grilled the instructor about the worthiness of focusing so much energy on competition. Wouldn't it be better to study how we could improve what we do from within our organisation?

This turned out to be a big lesson in 'consider the source'. That particular instructor was teaching from a state of fear. He was in the midst of losing his business due to other companies offering similar training. When I suggested he contact his competitors to see if they could work together, he looked at me like I was insane!

I know now that two heads (or more!) are better than one. Being a bit naïve at the time, I listened to the instructor's lousy advice and steered away from what my gut was telling me. Over the next several years, I monitored other companies like I was a hunter. Anyone else who offered similar services to my company- it was my job to take them down like a lioness. Not only did this approach lead to poor results, but it also made me reach burn out.

Imagine me, the head of our organisation, maintaining such high levels of distaste, distrust and attention focused solely on the competition. No surprise we didn't achieve our targets or grow for those three years. Now imagine if I had directed that attention IN HOUSE. Something had to change.

I decided to stop butting up against a competitive brick wall. I needed a different lens so I started looking at other companies differently. I viewed the similarities and differences, examining how we served customers in different ways...all of a sudden the word "opportunity" lit up my brain like a neon sign at dusk.

Opportunities to expand, work together, and refer one another. The first time I gave it a crack, it worked well. The other company head could see my vision, and she too felt it was a way to offer an even better service. Boom.

In 12 months, I took the sales from one of our businesses from $1 million to $1.8 million. We cut costs and increased efficiencies in warehouse and admin teams. Later I continued this ethos and in the role of General Manager, I took a national organisation from 400 clients to over 4000 clients in a possible pool of 7000. That meant more than half the available market was with my company!

In another business, I took sales from $100,000 turnover to over $1.9million.

If the numbers could talk, they would tell you this resulted from collaboration and connection via community. The businesses grew, not because of my ideas but because I listened to others. I asked my 'competition' if they wanted to work with me to develop together.

In the corporate world, this is far from typical practice but within our organisation, giving the teams opportunities to connect and communicate with one another showed that we could improve upon good ideas and the best would emerge. What a concept! I proved this approach works in five other organisations and taught countless others how to do the same.

I interrupt my flow here to show you two examples way outside of what I personally engaged to encourage collaboration instead of competition.

Alexander Graham Bell said, "Great discoveries and improvements invariably involve the cooperation of many minds." If he had not believed such, Bell would not have invented the telephone, created the American Bell Corporation and its successor, AT&T. This would not have been possible if not for his collaboration with Thomas A Watson.

Although Watson was technically Bell's 'employee,' Watson's ideas and electrical expertise were integral to the telephone systems back then and even of what we still use today. Had this collaboration not happened, maybe we wouldn't be addicted to the tiny devices in our pockets!

And another example, small towns. They tend to be tightly-knit business communities, and this is evident in their shopping districts. If there are two stores selling shoes, I would bet on it that they will not stock the same brands. The shop owners simply need to place a phone call to make sure they aren't competing for the same dollars.

Say this small town has a hat store; it's doubtful another hat store will pop up and try to take over the market by putting the original store out of business. That would be uncool, and shoppers would be loyal to the first hat shop owner anyway - he or she is their neighbour, in-law or friend!

In my hypothetical small-town shopping village, these people communicate with one another, especially during tough times; just like reality right now, in a post COVID world. It benefits the entire community to collaborate, let ideas flow back and forth and allow everyone to stay in business. Gestures of goodwill often benefit both the giver and receiver. In this way, in a small town in small locally owned stores, they can all bounce back after a downturn and we can all still have the services we love at our fingertips!

When I combine the small town business lessons with my personal experience, I've learned two things.

One is that as a leader, I will always cherish other people's opinions and ideas.

Two is that even if I disagree or didn't think of something myself, I will treat those opinions and ideas with great respect.

You have to consider all opinions and ideas to allow yourself to expand and grow. You never know where the next great idea will come from. It might take your business up a notch, streamline your admin, give you more time or make your income soar.

In a digital marketplace, we are connected to each other in ways that were impossible in the past. We have access to information about people and places around us through social media platforms and the web. The Internet makes it easier to access an infinite network and connects us with others who share our interests and passions. Find these people! Build those communities! Approach these tasks with abundance, not a scarcity mindset. There are more than enough customers to go around - so let's help lift one another up!

I wanted to list for you in a practical sense what some of these collaborations might look like with a digital business...

- **Affiliate programs** – where one promotes another and receives a payment for any sign-ups.
- **Working together on a set project** – a one-off project where you work together until said project is completed.
- **Market research** – asking specific questions and getting feedback from your ideal market – reward them at project conclusion.
- **Swap communities** – you might do an interview or presentation to each other's communities or an email to each other's list.
- **Combining resources** – pool the best of what you've got and combine forces.
- **Freebies** – to encourage others to learn and grow and expand without expectation of any return.

The best way to find and contribute to collaborations is to be open to the possibilities that the Universe (God, Spirit, Fate, Guides – whatever your choice of description is,) presents for you. Most people are set in their ways and are adverse to change, especially if things are working well enough. But imagine what it could feel like to take your work to the next level! All you have to do is keep a flexible mindset and be open to change.

Possibilities...

- we do not know where they might take us,
- we do not know who might lead us to them,
- we do not know how they will impact our lives!

Through the incredible power of possibility, I found myself open to forming my own publishing house.

This move was the correct business decision for me in terms of my energy, output and wellbeing. Now I collaborate with women daily through the power of storytelling and we launch those gifts into the world to inspire others. It is purposeful and the best use of my skills and experience.

I am often approached to collaborate on new book ideas and I love this. What an honour it is to be part of helping others carve out their legacy in the world. But books are not the only way to collaborate - I consciously am and have to remain open to all the other possibilities within the realm this world.

As I'm writing this, the collaboration I'm most excited about is my opportunity to be the guest trainer for a Writers Retreat in Italy. It takes place in November 2022 – fully organised, flights, accommodation, location, memorable daily travel with a host to idyllic locations, divine food for myself and 10 special guests. What a joy to be offered such an opportunity!

Do you want this story to be yours? Or something similar? Because it can be.

If you're busy in the seat of competition, in the seductive hustle rollercoaster; Look up! Just for a second. I want to point out a few things for you.

COMPETITION IS NOT UNLIKE COMPARISON

Now you might be thinking I am stretching to prove these concepts are similar but hear me out...

The dictionary notes the origin of competition is from the Latin word *competere* which means *"to strive for"*.

Where the word comparison originated the Latin word *comparatio* meaning "to pair, match".

There's nothing wrong with seeing someone a few steps ahead of you and being inspired to lift your game. I just worry that this 'friendly' competitive spirit can get too dark at times and stop serving us.

I know you would have heard this saying, "Comparison is the thief of joy." How true it is. So I ask you to ponder on these questions...

When you compare yourself to your competition:

Are you jealous?

Do you want to take over?

Maybe, just maybe you can consider working together so you can share joy's trophy?

I have no intention of slowing down but I do not hustle. Let me repeat that; I DO Not HUSTLE. Collaborations come in with ease and grace because I allow the energy to flow to me and through me. I am open to partnerships and will take the initiative to ask for them too. It all comes down to the three C's; Community, Connection and Collaboration.

For a moment, think about children- before society gets a chance to stamp, collect and place them into categories. In a group situation, children naturally collaborate for the better of the group as a whole. They don't judge, compare and analyse the size and structure of one another's building blocks. They'd rather pool resources, build the biggest tower and take turns smashing it.

Instead of being in competition, we should consider that it takes a village to make a business grow, just like a child.

It's starting to happen. I see it online. Many people, particularly women, strive to create businesses out of their passion and aren't doing it alone. They are taking their sisters along for the ride. The very movement "rise sister rise" is so commonplace that is becoming the standard rather than the exception.

By sharing the work, we can achieve so much more.

If you take the practical (a bigger pool of ideas give you more options) and the spiritual (connection of self to community) your possibilities for expansion are limitless.

WHERE TO START?

You might not know where to start and if that's how you feel, I recommend starting with yourself. You must listen to your intuition and guidance before you can consider allowing others to guide you. Get quiet and learn how to hear your inner voice, it might be a whisper at first but like a muscle, it gets stronger the more you use it. Before long, that intuition becomes a compass for every decision you make in life and in business.

Living in a competitive, comparative state is actually you living in fear. And I think we all know by now that making decisions from a place of fear will never give the same results as making decisions from a place of security and trust.

The good news is that you can overcome your fear, just like you can overcome your social, cultural, religious and/or other experiences that may give you a bias.

Businesses could learn a lot from children's playgroups- think of it as having a start-up mindset. Take risks, talk to your competitors, share ideas, collaborate to build something that serves your customers better and most essential is to have fun!

In the end, do you want to squabble for every dollar, waste energy on judgement, comparison or compete or do you want to provide the most kick-ass product or service possible and make your customers the happiest? Collaboration is where the magic happens!

What's your legacy?

Yours in Community Spirit,
B xx

ABOUT THE AUTHOR

BRIGID HOLDER

Brigid Holder is the CEO of The Art of Grace Publishing House, their vision is to share the stories of women internationally, granting permission for others to change their lives whilst impacting the writer.

During her successful senior management roles in the corporate world, Brigid and her husband launched their own traditional business that is today a thriving 17 year-old organisation where she holds the role of Company Director.

As an USA TODAY and international best-selling author Brigid found the power of storytelling and is passionate to share and showcase this for other women.

Brigid operates both businesses alongside her husband and their two teenage boys from a small rural town in Australia.

The publishing house has two international best-selling books; INTUITIVE and F@#* Motherhood, several more coming soon.

"Through writing we are creatively releasing past trauma and in doing so, we allow others the permission to do the same." Brigid Holder

Website: https://brigidholder.com/
Facebook: https://www.facebook.com/BrigidAuthorPublisher

CLAUDIA SPAHR

THE ART OF HOLDING SPACE AND WHY CIRCLE IS MEDICINE FOR OUR TIME

WELCOME!

I'd like to invite you to come on a journey with me.

Get comfortably seated, and then take your hands and lift the flesh of your buttocks and spread them across your seat. Can you feel your connection to the earth below you? At this point I stick out my behind like a Fertility Goddess because it feels juicy, powerful and grounded. If you're a man, you also have an inner Fertility Goddess. She likes to wrap herself around your scrotum and give it a gentle but provocative squeeze.

Are you ready?

Let's go!

We are going to have an experience. Let's call it an experiment. Humans need to experiment because that is a great way to assimilate new understanding. We can truly grow and expand by moving out of our comfort zones.

In this experiment, I'm using the technique of circle and the art of holding space to make my point. Let us explore how this works.

Wherever you are now seated, look around you and take in your surroundings. Do you know where the sun is right now? Where South, North, East and West are? If it is night-time, where did the sun set and where will the moon rise?

Now imagine observing yourself via the camera lens of a drone just above you. Using your mind's eye, fly that drone further up and out. Watch as you get smaller and smaller. Are you able to take in more of the surroundings, situating your position on the planet? Can you see your village, town or city, then your country? You might be a visual person and find this really easy, or you might be able to imagine it conceptually. There is no right or wrong way to do this.

I call this my Google Earth trick and it helps me get the 360° perspective. It allows me to feel the vast nature of my being and how interconnected everything is.

I see beauty in every direction. I see potential in every direction. I am like the eagle or the condor, taking it all in.

Some people spend a lot of time dwelling on the past. Others are more focused on the future; planning and often worrying about things that may or may not happen. The French Renaissance philosopher, Michel de Montaigne, famously said: "My life has been filled with terrible misfortune; most of which never happened." Recent studies show that up to 97% of peoples' imagined misfortunes never occur.

Being firmly rooted in the here and now is a powerful vantage point. Allow yourself to truly experience what it is like to be fully present to the moment.

Doing this is quintessential to the art of holding space, so that you can fully witness and hear others. The age-old wisdom of circle is a tried and tested tool for community connection, as each voice is honoured in a non-judgemental way. Holding space is a softening into a neutral and receptive stance without any attachments. Leading a circle, I ease into an open, non-egoic, right-brained state that requires steady presence and grounded strength. I trust and surrender to the process and the energy of the group dynamics. As the initiator, by bringing my attention into my heart, others are given the prompt to let go of control. Through this connection we are able to take on an open, unconditional perspective that allows us to be part of the solution and transform any conflicts or limiting beliefs.

Humans need rituals, systems, and common agreements in order to understand what is at stake and effectively get things done. Hence we ritualise the process of sitting together in circle. It allows us to co-create a container with very clear boundaries. The clearer the boundaries, the greater the communion.

Take some moments to breathe this wisdom down through your body into your belly. Set your intention for the next few minutes. What would you like to gain, learn or know from reading these paragraphs? I will set the intention to describe in words - in the simplest and most direct way possible - why sitting in circle is a great medicine for our times.

Now we have co-created a virtual container, across time and space, without even being physically present with each other. Isn't that wonderful?

THIS IS WHAT IT MEANS TO LIVE AND WORK IN COOPERATIVE MUTUAL UNDERSTANDING

Co-creating an intentional space, grounds, centres, and unites the group. By protecting this space we invoke the sacred. We can consciously co-create sacred moments with life anytime and anywhere; via intention, affirmative words, authenticity and feelings. All of us are vibrational energy manifested in physical form. An experienced space holder will touch the hearts and minds of every single person in the circle, allowing an alchemical process for those present honouring the guidelines and sacredness of it.

Now let us call in the directions. If you didn't know where North was before, take a moment to check. Most phones have an inbuilt compass app.

I've been hosting hundreds of international live events for a diverse range of people from all over the world since 2008. No group or retreat is ever the same. Beginning a retreat week with an Opening Circle allows me the opportunity to feel into each new group. What I do on my Ibiza retreats is call in directions by giving them a simple map of the beaches of the island. HolyMama retreats attract a mixed audience and I want everyone to feel included with practical instructions. The spiritual can remain unforced and subtle.

¨Behind me we have the beautiful sandy eastern beaches of Aguas Blancas and Es Figueral. To the South (pointing) you will find Ibiza town and beyond that Las Salinas and Es Cavallet. If you drive West, towards the sunset .....etc".

Why do I use the directions to open space? Because it is part of this age-old practice. It has been used by indigenous, earth-based cultures and traditions from all corners of the planet since the beginning of time. I tend to use the South American Shamanic tradition of the Quechua. I mix it up with my ancestral Celtic lineage and other traditions.

LET US BEGIN IN THE NORTH

I invite you to open up to this ancient part of yourself that knows what you know.

"Hail and welcome North and the guardians of the watchtowers of the North. Bring spirit and the element of air into our sacred space to bless and refresh us with its original mystery. May this soft breeze blow out the cobwebs of maya in our minds, so that we can think and see clearly the matters at hand. Let the winds of change lift us up, so that like the eagle we can see everything from a higher and more complete perspective. And like the condor who has the lightest heart of all the spirit animals, may we release and transform any sorrows, imprints, conditioning or heavy burdens, as we enter this sacred space."

During this guided experience with you, I shall use the directions as placeholders for stories. Each direction will tell a story to illustrate a point.

THE STORY FOR NORTH

It takes place during the Cold War, in the mid-1980s. The US and Russia are competing in a dangerous arms race of medium range nuclear missiles. U.S. President Reagan and Russia's General Secretary Gorbachev meet on the shores of Lake Geneva for a high-level summit, in an attempt to ease the relations between the two nations. Initially it seems to go nowhere because the men have conflicting views and deep mistrust of one another. Reagan is an actor-turned-president who worships the ethos of capitalism and the other, a committed communist, seen by the West as the leader of an "evil empire". Not only are they in opposition, but they sit with their delegations at a long table opposite each other. They battle it out in antagonistic meetings that end in a stalemate with mutual insults of 'dinosaur' and 'hard-headed Bolshevik'. Things take a turn when they decide to break from negotiations and go for a walk to air their heads, with only their private interpreters present. They walk together, side by side, both facing and moving in the same direction. This walk in the woods, near the lakeside Villa Fleur d'Eau, enables a breakthrough and marks the beginning of a friendship that will end the nuclear tension between the world's two most powerful nations.

Notice how this anecdote illustrates how important our physical positioning is. When we are next to each other, we are on the same side. In circle we are always next to somebody. There are not two sides but one flowing circular form, without any breaks. The conversation moves around the circle, as the talking stick is passed from one to another (the talking stick can be a physical object but needn't be). There is a natural and organic flow as everyone has a chance to be heard.

LET US NOW TURN TO THE EAST

You can face that way now, if you like.

"Hail and welcome East. We honour the East, turning to the rising sun and all that is rising in us: Our fire, our creativity, our passion. As fertile beings, may we own our sexuality and use it wisely to create and co-create with life. May the spirit animals that know of the fires before they burn, guide us and may the stealth of the panther as he stalks the forests bless us with his alert instinct."

This next story is about a designer. She is talented and creative, and has built up her reputation over decades, working hard as a woman in a male dominated profession while fitting her work around motherhood. The scene takes place inside an architects' office, where our designer is presenting updated plans she has drawn up for a multi-million Euro project they're working on. The men on her team recognise the merits of her work, but instead of celebrating her, they feel threatened and tear her down. They troll her, undermining her integrity as a professional and questioning her status as self-employed. One of her colleagues comments that *his* wife gave up her job to stay at home and focus on the children. In spite of this harassment, the project goes on to be approved by their clients, and the designer is lauded for her impeccable and original work.

The above mansplaining, gaslighting and chauvinism is still common everywhere around the world. Whether blatant or subtle, aggression is frequently used against women, people of colour and minorities by those of privilege. Patriarchal misbehaviour festers in unsafe and hostile environments. It creates separation and unhealthy competition.

If the future is to be collaborative (and I believe it is the only viable future) then we need to evolve a more integrated and balanced form of leadership that breaks down the hierarchical power structures of domination and control. We need to give everyone a voice and a seat at the table. We need to include and diversify. It will make the world a much more accepting place to live in. Part of our evolution as a species is moving towards more diversity, complexity and refinement. These next decades are key to the survival of the human race and we will need to use discernment to make wise choices. We either steer the ship on a different course or we sail blindly ahead into the most violent storm the world has ever seen.

As the Dalai Lama famously said: “If you think you’re too small to make a difference, try sleeping with a mosquito.”

LET US TURN NOW TO THE SOUTH

Here we can centre and ground what we have thus experienced:

“Hail South and welcome to the earth, rocks and stones. Pachamama, our great Mother, we honour you and call on the majestic Apus of South America, Table Mountain, Kilimanjaro, Ayers Rock, Mount Kailash, Mount Shasta and all the other sacred mountains that grace our planet to support us in our daily lives. May our experiences be embodied gracefully, so that we can walk this earth with dignity and reverence for the bountiful gifts Mother Earth provides to nourish us. Like the serpent, may we renew by shedding our outdated skin”.

For this next story I turn to my retreats to give you an example of how important it is to be grounded in your mission and vision. One of the great learnings I have received over the last years is how to stay true to my path, without being distracted, bullied or pulled in directions that lead to me ‘leaking energy’. Energetic states can be sabotaged by others. If you are not clear with your intentions, words and deeds, you can be taken out by chaotic forces.

This incident takes place during 2016, during my fourth year of running the HolyMama retreats. We are growing steadily and retreats are fully booked without having to advertise them. Due to increased demand I have to rent extra houses to accommodate the number of mothers and children who want to attend. One of the houses isn't our first choice, but I have a wonderful, heart-led team supporting my vision and we spend a couple of days 'pimping it up', so it's comfortable and safe for the mums and kids.

I notice her antagonism already in the opening circle. Motherhood is the biggest transformative change in a woman's life and when women come to us, some are struggling. This particular mother is angry. Angry at her situation, her job, her family and the world around her. In a safe space we never judge anyone and one of the guidelines I use for the retreats is: "Never judge a mother until you have walked a mile in her shoes." As things evolve, the first impression I had of this woman makes sense towards the end of the retreat, when she starts complaining about her accommodation. She recruits two other mothers to back her up in projecting her pent up anger onto me and a few months later she sends an email on their behalf, demanding a full refund for a retreat they had all completed. This experience leads me to work on my personal sovereignty and deepen my studies into shamanic practices, space holding and circle, so that this kind of emotional sabotage can be dealt with from a more grounded and loving place.

It inspires my creation of the 'HolyMama LoveField'. This is an intention we set before the retreat begins and we ground it in the Opening Circle. I explain to the new group how we are holding the frequency for everyone who enters the space. Thanks to this clear container, those present can fully and authentically express themselves. This means that powerful transformation evolves naturally. I've come to understand that deep healing occurs more effortlessly when women connect with each other and themselves. The HolyMama LoveField protects the group from being overwhelmed by the negative state of any individual present. It takes a very flexible, adaptable and strong system to hold and support about 20 mothers plus 20 young children living together for a week. This is what circle provides.

LET US FINALLY TURN TO THE WEST

"We call in the element of water, the moon and our intuitive nature. I would like to honour the finned ones - the dolphins, the whales, the mermaids and all the mythical creatures of the oceans. May our compassion be all encompassing and may our senses attune to the mystical nature of our being."

For the last example we look at conflict management and team restoration. I've been hired to resolve a corporate dispute that is hampering working relationships and leading to high absenteeism and reduced productivity. The employees feel threatened by two of the managers and the managers are afraid of losing their jobs. It is a toxic and unsafe working environment for all.

Before bringing the teams and managers together for a one-day seminar, I prepare the room, setting the intention to "clear the air" (this can also be done for virtual seminars). The participants enter the space to relaxing music. We open the circle with short introductions and share our favourite weekend pastimes. This connects everyone on the same human level and gives each a voice. The morning continues with smaller break-out circles. I deliberately separate the management and teams who usually work together. They are assigned different problems to solve and some team building exercises. The atmosphere of fun collaboration and support is built up throughout the morning. By the afternoon we are ready to address more complex and relevant issues from their everyday reality. The ´silent´ employees feel safe to voice their concerns and suggest ways to increase productivity. These ideas are celebrated and built on by other employees, and the dynamic shifts. By the end of the day the two managers commit to making changes after having seen that solutions can come from within the team. This is power from the centre, rather than top-down force.

Circle allows us to share power together from within and lead from the centre, eliminating the need of the destructive power structures that have dominated the world for thousands of years. When communication is circular, delegation feels naturally organic and responsibility becomes collective.

Before we close space, I'd like to talk about the importance of feeling safe. Think back to the Palaeolithic era when humans would gather in a circle around the fire. They would be able to see any potential danger approaching from all sides. Everyone had everyone's back. This perfect and simple form of circle created safety for them.

When we feel unsafe we become afraid. This causes stress in the body and the nervous system. Our world feels very unsafe for millions on the planet who are experiencing war, poverty, corrupt systems and a sense of doom due to climate change. On top of that we have the Covid 19 pandemic adding to the sense that we are in danger wherever we go.

We are living in a traumatised world, and there has never been a greater need to create safe spaces that provide nourishment, healing and collaborative opportunities. I would even go so far to say that mental and physical health and wellness are the currency now. They should be top of the agenda for politicians and the decisions we make in our economies.

Thank you for your time. Thank you for your presence. May you be well, may you be loved, may your heart be as light as a condor's feather, so that you recognise what is real and true.

I release the directions to the West, South, East and North.

May the circle be open, yet unbroken.

ABOUT THE AUTHOR

CLAUDIA SPAHR

Claudia Spahr is a #1 international best-selling author, inspirational speaker, business leadership mentor and global pioneer in the retreat and wellness industry. She is the award-winning founder and CEO of HolyMama. Claudia has trained retreat leaders in over 20 countries, across 6 continents and hosted hundreds of transformational retreats across the world, using circle principles to motivate diverse, pop-up teams. She has been heralded as a wellness leader by the Guardian, Telegraph, Huffington Post and Psychologies Magazine. Disrupt ranked HolyMama as the #1 Retreat Company and Business Growth Catalyst for Mothers. Previously Claudia worked as a radio broadcast journalist and TV foreign correspondent. She is mama to two boys and a girl, whom she birthed in her forties.

You can find more about Claudia's retreats, books, and online leadership trainings at http://holymama.info/ and http://claudiaspahr.com/

Get in touch or invite her to speak and motivate your employees or your community: admin@holymama.info

Social media
Instagram: https://www.instagram.com/_holymama_/
Facebook: https://www.facebook.com/holymamaretreats
LinkedIn: https://www.linkedin.com/in/claudia-spahr-42220a8/

SEAN MOLONEY

IMMUTABLE COLLECTIVISM & EMPOWERED COLLABORATION ON THE BLOCKCHAIN

It has been a long road since 1971 when the world's economies shifted on their axis via a 'temporary' removal of currency off the gold standard as previously ordained at Bretton Woods. Since then, the world has become hooked on its own ability to seemingly remedy any economic, social, geographical, political or moral dystopia on the unfettered ability to simply print more and more fiat currency. Often at the whim of a few decision makers within government and central banks. A fiat currency is money that is not backed by a physical commodity like gold, but instead backed by the government that issued it. Most modern currencies, such as the U.S. dollar, euro, pound, and yen are fiat money. "Fiat" means "an authoritative or arbitrary order" and has no ability to protect purchasing power.

Appreciating the difference between money and currency highlights the challenges this can bring to societies. Simply, money is designed to protect your purchasing power, currency is not. In my case it was a lesson learned in the 2008 Great Recession and led to a decade-long journey of investigation, not only into why fiat currency was not serving society, but also what alternatives exist for the government-issued means of exchange. Especially one rife with middlemen, fees and vested interest.

First of all it begs the question: Why do most people spend so much of a lifetime exchanging time and skill for currency?

The answer is as complex as it is interesting. A potent mix of perception management and a lack of financial education. The needs fiat has as a debt-based system and big government hooked on its own inability to create borrowing in the face of four-year power cycles, as opposed to encouraging any real sustainable value in the economy.

The modern world has been built on the premise of borrowed currency based on the bonds, stocks and currency issuance of a few centralized institutions now 'too big to fail', as proven in the 2008 financial shock.

Did the 2008 warning trigger an introspective look into the way the financial system had been allowed to develop since 1971, the year the world entered a full fiat system? Did the money men see the error of their ways in providing lending to those in no position to service or repay the debt? Did the governments of the world take this crash as evidence we need a better way? Do the governments, a decade on, work to redistribute wealth and protect the people from unsustainable debt?

It seems not. Rather the largest economies of the world prefer to maintain the fiat system regardless of the consequences to quality of life, the unbanked, people's life chances, or the sheer level of debt being passed on to our grandchildren.

Whether blockchain and associated tokenisation of value (often called "crypto currencies") can provide a viable alternative, time will tell.

The last decade has proven what is possible when the technology is used to galvanise people onto immutable and trustless systems of ownership and utility. A unique function of blockchain that has my attention is the phenomenon of shared ownership that leads to wealth redistribution, which is available now in 2021. We are focused on sharing this knowledge and information so others can begin to participate. Let's explore more of the background and real life solutions in this chapter.

IGNORANT OR COMPLICIT?

If those in power won't (or can't) provide the top-down honesty and policy to create a level playing field for mankind, who can?

The era of conforming collectivism v. democratic individualism is now over 100 years old, the product of converging ideologies determined to establish their brand of human existence. Which has proven to be the best method remains up for debate. What is clear is both are proving their ability to create a widening wealth gap in their populations as we head to the middle of the 21st century.

So, what next? What has the last 100 years given us as a foundation to build the next century in a manner more conducive to equality, opportunity for all and human betterment?

Healthcare, education, travel, sanitation, security, arguably, are better for most. But at what cost? Seven billion mouths need feeding. These same people need sustaining.Can our planet continue to serve at this rate?

If not, the cost could be much higher than mere finances, but is the lack of financial balance part of the root cause of this cost? Could the imbalance in human use of the planet be financial as more and more people find ways to exploit each other?

Many would suggest so, but again, what is being done? Are our leaders' platitudes acceptable in four-year cycles of hope that someone, or some party will break the mold? How many decades do we allow a downward effect for most people?

A decade ago this question may have been open to debate, a process of society's accepted evolution.

By 2021, in a post-Covid19 world, it seems less so. A decade of austerity for most already lived, a wealth gap wider than ever, more unbanked people than ever in human history and a sense the baby boomers were a zenith of human existence.

A decade ago, quantitative easing was unheard of. "Too big to fail" financial institutions were still being fathomed. The dollar-based fiat system's ability to hang on no matter what, was underestimated.

A decade ago, a technology designed to put means of exchange, wealth preservation, transparency and immutable assurance was little understood.

A decade ago, Bitcoin was just entering the human global psyche.

BLOCKCHAIN – WHY IS IT RELEVANT?

Cryptography, the basis for blockchain as we know it, is not a new concept.

The invention of a use case designed to provide every person on the planet access to an immutable, accurate, trustless store of value is.

In 2009 a scientific white paper was released into the world detailing a concept that utilized blockchain technology to provide an alternate means of exchange based on the internet, and with inherent ability to be fixed in supply, yet unlimited in demand. Bitcoin was introduced to the world.

Most dismissed it, quick to follow the narrative of their education, parents, bosses, banks and governments that alternate means of people exchanging value had to be a fad. Once it proved not to be it was derided as a scam, only suitable for drug runners and speculators working against the system.

By 2017 Bitcoin was valued at over $16 000 per coin. The retail money (read currency) piled in, then the whales (large holders of digital currency) gorged on greed and fear.

All the while the institutions were continuing to dismiss the technology – or more specifically Bitcoin – while at the same time developing their own blockchain use cases.

By 2019 the likes of VISA, Mastercard, PayPal, et al were publicly endorsing their backing of blockchain. By 2020 the institutions had moved on acquiring Bitcoin.

In less than a decade the blockchain industry developed into a 10 000+ project entity, valued at over $2 TRILLION1. Some of the best-known industries, organizations and brands directly or indirectly developed versions of themselves "on chain".

Moreover, next-generation companies were being born determined to disrupt the decades-old systems of centralization, top-down control, the wealthy few and the middlemen fees.

All the while, ordinary individuals were acquiring ownership of the technology and funding the growth of these next-generation industries and organizations.

Decentralisation was being born right in front of our eyes. The concept that millions of people could collaborate to create disruption, efficiency, cost reduction, wealth redistribution, and a means of protecting purchasing power was in play.

THE AGE OF THE EMPOWERED COLLABORATION

So, what next?

Where will a technology designed to redistribute wealth, provide all with decentralized means of exchange, and most of all, empower the participants therein take us?

On the face of it today most seem intent on speculating and driving endless YouTube chatter about the latest coin or when bitcoin will hit $100 000 per coin.

In fact, the technology fundamentals are much more nuanced than that.

For over a decade the technology has matured, layer on layer of deeper use cases, arguably hitting an early high-water mark with a concept called 'decentralized finance' or Defi.

A true revolution in how wealth is managed, created and distributed? Time will tell. or now we understand its potential for providing every individual on the planet a platform on which to acquire, own, collateralize, grow and manage assets that either have value on their own utility, or represent a digitalised version of something of value.

This means that the world's wealth can be re-distributed. Every household can become sovereign or at least financially empowered.

A pipe dream? Or a brave new world?

Only a journey into what we know today can provide some insight into Defi's potential, a potential built on several layers of technology that are already actively available today.

THE ROLE OF ETHEREUM

Ethereum (ETH) was conceived by 19-year-old, Russian-Canadian, computer science geek and *Bitcoin Magazine* writer, Vitalik Buterin in November 2013. Buterin's white paper, written after three years spent exploring the emerging crypto sector, was his response to the limitations of Bitcoin, and proposed a platform enabling any decentralized, censorship-resistant application imaginable.

It has become the layer-ne technology of a phenomenon known as 'Smart Contracts', a fully-automated, immutable and transparent mechanism of certainty on any given business process, system or exchange agreement. The world is slowly waking up to this technology's possibilities.

Most of the 10 000 blockchain applications (coins) that make up the coin market cap directory are based on Ethereum's native protocol – ERC20. Thus, providing a huge upside to the utility of ETH even at this very early stage. Most large institutions and organisations in the world are yet to deploy its efficiencies and cost-reducing credentials into their operations.

Extraordinary leaps in the way people interact and manage everyday activities, business dealings and government organisation are on the horizon, with Ethereum blockchain technology set at the heart of that change.

SMART CONTRACTS ARE BORN

In the meantime, as is the usual adoption pattern of all new technologies, it is the innovators and those seeking to gain an edge on the market that are the early adopters. Industry sectors as diverse as education to charity, electricity supply to banking, and trading platforms to gaming are all developing next-generation use cases for their services and utilities. With one significant difference: This time, it is not the banking systems or venture capital industry funding their start-up activities. It's the collaboration of the crowd, known as Crowdfund 2.0 in blockchain circles.

The very nature of immutable, personal and transparent ownership of digital assets (coins) lends itself to a new phenomenon where thousands of individuals capitalise start-ups in exchange for tokens or coins on the blockchain that are then held by the private individual. The company's utility is nurtured, and the "coin" creates equity over time via supply and demand, as well as an income from the activities of the start-up platform over time.

In other words, blockchain technology is providing the structure on which people can take direct ownership of business functions from anywhere in the world, with immutable and certain ownership of digital assets that are directly tied to the value the business function involves.

As these new companies evolve, further demand is placed on the coin supply, and demand economies are created. As traditional industry sees the shift, the technology is further adopted. Over time centralised, stock-market-driven ownership is disrupted.

Let's look at some real-world examples of this in action.

PowerLedger www.powerledger.io

Powerledger, an Australian based blockchain enterprise, has developed an energy and flexibility trading platform that allows households, organisations and the grid, itself, to trade with each other.

Traditionally solar panel technologies exist in isolation, with any excess power not used by the user being sold back to the centralised power grid to be used elsewhere.

PowerLedger adjusts this dynamic by allowing solar panel users to connect via the blockchain and trade power with each other directly. They are shifting renewable energy from a centralised system in isolation to a redistributed system where households, businesses and private users of solar technology can monetise the sun, itself.

Helium www.helium.com

Powered by the Helium Blockchain, The People's Network represents a paradigm shift for decentralized wireless infrastructure. They claim to be starting a wireless revolution where individual households and businesses create the necessary infrastructure, collaborating to remove the need for centralized infrastructure. Instead, households create the necessary network of wireless devices in 3-mile quadrants. By deploying a simple device in your home or office, you can provide your city with miles of low-power network coverage for billions of devices and earn a cryptocurrency, HNT for doing so.

SuperOne www.super.one

One of the first gaming companies to combine the worlds of mobile gaming and social sharing with blockchain technology infrastructure. Players participate in general knowledge-based games in sport, travel, celebrity, and food, acquiring credits to play as per many mobile games in the world today. The difference however is that participants are rewarded in XRP in real time taking a share in the total revenues being created by players and advertisers.

Equally interesting is the use of smart contracts to create Non-Fungible Tokens (NFTs) where SuperOne participants are able to acquire these tokens and lease them to other game players as they look for the information held on them in game. An early example of monetization of NFTs.

RealT www.realt.co

"Fractional and frictionless real estate investing". Investors around the globe can buy into the real estate market through fully compliant, fractional, tokenized ownership via the blockchain. An interesting model of collaboration by dozens of individuals to capitalize property ownership in the residential rental space. Rental revenues are then redistributed to the owners, via smart contract, on a weekly basis.

These are new ways to create value, to redistribute that value and digital asset ownership to individuals - people who collaborate in everyday activities. This is arguably the fundamental function of blockchain as a technology.

THE FUTURE OF MONEY

One of the most interesting areas of empowered collaboration on blockchain technology is the world of finance. The relentless pursuit of fiat currency to be the default method of human exchange of value may well be looked back on as a time of inevitable monetary experimentation that did not serve the greater good of human societies. So, what is the future of money?

We gain a glimpse of possibility by combining the aspects we have discussed in this chapter, namely blockchain technology itself, subsequent smart contracts and decentralized finance. Just as with the redistribution of solar power, communication networks or gaming revenues to players, the other major use case for blockchain is the banking system itself.

For generations central banks have been the purveyor of the monetary system—a privilege cemented into the trajectory of human society back in 1913 with the incarnation of the Federal Reserve. The world has become what it has become, a series of booms and busts until the inevitable move to a full fiat system in 1971. The 50 years since then has seen a population explosion in humankind, with an equivalent explosion in currency issuance, and hence world debt.

As we begin the third decade of the 21st Century the established decision makers seem intent to continue to operate under this monetary model, despite billions being unbanked and the banked feeling increasingly underwhelmed by the nature of their energy and skills providing them purchasing power they can rely on for a lifetime.

Pension funds are woefully underfunded and headed for crisis in the next decade as Boomers and GenX turn to their children and grandchildren to provide the funds of their old age. A fundamental issue, given the falling birth rate since the 1980's. An issue compounded by the fiat system's inherent inability to protect purchasing power. Savers are losers, lost in the advice of the fund managers, financial advisers and middle men that a lifetime of giving your capital to others was better than owning your own assets. Why? One word: Fees.

Do we see a fundamental change being created by the monetary scientists on how people can ensure fair return on their energy and skill—especially as they enter old age? Or do we see yet another spin on the same fiat system?

Early this decade 'central bank digital currencies (CBDC's) are in the works from China to the USA, a concept with no relation to the attributes of blockchain, being simply an extension of the fiat system in a computer-connected age. A new Bretton Woods is underway as the world adjusts to a post-Covid19 era.

What the future holds for our concept of money is to be seen, but one idea may well be born not of the top-down policy makers, but of the people themselves.

As decentralized finance increases in its legitimacy and relevance in the financial system, people are beginning to realize how they can in fact take back some level of control, to own assets. A strange concept indeed, given the hundreds of years centralized businesses have maintained control of ownership and currency issuance. The phenomenon that each individual and household owns assets that are then collateralized to society via the blockchain, thus creating "fee" incomes to the people (as opposed to the banks and associated middlemen) is underway.

People then use this income to live life by spending in the same society activities that leveraged the assets. Simply, the technology is used to allow individuals to collaborate on a global basis via the redistribution of inherent wealth already held in society.

A concept yet to be fully understood, however as more and more use cases develop and mature in the use of blockchain and its ability to encourage collaboration it will be interesting to see if people vote with their feet away from the centralized banking systems and toward decentralized means of ownership and exchange.

For sure, the future will be navigated via the exponential rise of technology; it has always been that way. Maybe this time blockchain technology will help people create the best of collectivism and individualism in a world that can only truly function in the spirit of empowered collaboration.

So what is being done in practical terms to provide this awareness to people? On our part at Digital Business Masters (www.digitalbusinessmasters.io) we have created an academy and consultancy based arm of our work to help individuals and businesses to take action in blockchain technology. Education is key at this stage.

A steady awareness is underway as people begin to recognise the technology for its fundamental value. Businesses in particular are seeing opportunities to reduce costs, improve security, grow into new markets and raise capital. Individuals are learning how to create real incomes through collaboration with others and applications connected globally on the blockchain.

In an ever-changing world the next decade will see a shift in how people interact, transact and react to an economic system that no longer serves the interests of the people. It will be the people who create the change based on education and applied collaboration. We are doing our part to help that process along via education, empowerment and decentralisation. We invite you to learn more.

1 Source: *CoinMarketCap*

ABOUT THE AUTHOR

SEAN MOLONEY

Sean Moloney started his career in the manufacturing industry, learning early on the need to own assets and create business systems that work for you. Later applying this into property before realising the potential of blockchain technology by 2013.

Since then, Sean has immersed himself into the blockchain space, focused on understanding the fundamentals and use cases of the technology in industry, as well as its ability to empower individuals via wealth redistribution.

Sean founded Digital Business Masters in 2015, now including a Blockchain Academy of over 20 coaches globally. They are focused on helping individuals and business owners understand and transition into blockchain technology.

Sean Moloney is married and a father of two based in the UK.

Learn more at www.digitalbusinessmasters.io

PART V

COLLABORATION WITH SPIRIT

COLLABORATION WITH THE DIVINE

WRITTEN BY A TEACHER OF THE DIVINE

Nothing You See Means Anything...

This is contrary to the Belief System of the Ego, the Ego Mantra... Seek outside of yourself, but never find... keep trying but never succeed," indeed, the continual Seeking and Chasing of Illusion, trying ever harder to find fulfilment outside of yourself.

It is certainly Impossible not to believe what you see... it is equally impossible however to see what you Do Not Believe.

It is the latter we are dealing with, for if you wish to find the Divine, collaborate with the Divine. . . you will need to see differently with Real Vision, and a change of Belief is needed for this "New Seeing" to occur.

Your eyes will not see the Divine, for they were made to look away from the Divine, to look outside of yourself and to keep looking, keep trying, seeking and seeing everywhere else and ultimately never succeed in finding.

Only your mind's eye can see the Divine, only your mind can feel the Divine and only your mind can collaborate with the Divine.

When your current Belief system is fully exchanged for the Divine's, the Real World will rise before your eyes.

Full Understanding only Comes with Full Experience. To Fully Understand what you are, a Son of the Divine, you will need to Fully Experience yourself as the Divine made you... no more or less than the Divine itself.

But while there is Belief in your mind to the contrary that experiences judgement, analysing, frustration, guilt, shame, anger and attempts to plan, goal set or manifest, raise your own state of frequency through meditation and the list goes on... your willingness is needed to change your mind.

And... Your Willingness is all that is needed. It is your willingness that is very useful to the Divine.

If you are Willing to hand over your Mind to the Divine, everything you think you know, everything you have ever been taught, everyone you have ever experienced, everything you have ever experienced, the past, future and present for all of time and space... and come with Holy Open Hands, the Divine will fully restore your mind to that which was created as It's Son, at such point the Collaboration will be complete in its entirety.

You cannot change your own Belief System, as you do not know what to change it to. You did not create your mind and so cannot restore it. You can, however, change your mind to choosing the Divine rather than the Ego... and this is all you can ever do in your Illusion.

There are Two Thought Systems of Belief offered to you in Every moment, and the cumulative results of your Willingness to follow One Thought System or the Other will be bestowed upon you. Following both, alternately, will only make you and your life erratic... this will continue until you choose one, or the other all of the time.

Accept that you must ultimately choose between Two Teachers, each teaching their own Thought system. Accept this fact with great willingness and the Rest will be done for you depending on where you place your Willingness.

Fear not if you find you have chosen the Ego and experience the results of that choosing, for it is always possible for you to change your mind and place your Willingness with the Divine again.

The Following Handovers are a process you can use to place your Willingness with the Divine until such time as choosing the Divine is automatic in your mind.

The Handovers are simple, take three deep breaths into your Tummy… then In your Mind say the following:

> **"Divine… I hand All of my Thoughts over to you now… In this Holy Instance… to do with… as you Wish"**

> **"Divine… I hand All of my Relationships over to you now… In this Holy Instance… to do with… as you see fit"**

With these two Handovers, there is nothing Blocked by you from the Divine entering… Relationships of course are your Relationships to Everyone and Everything: the air you breathe, the Light you see, everything. 'Thoughts', of course are all of your Ideas, Plans for your life, Goals, Analysis, everything you think you know and have been taught previously. In letting go of all of your ideas, you will come to realise you give up nothing and are given everything in its place.

You are not "Surrendering" to the Divine, this would infer the giving up of your Willingness. Willingness you keep and is respected by the Divine with the Freedom of choice, always. What you are choosing with the Divine is to follow the only Truth, surely leading you home.

Currently you are Lost, Homeless and do not know anything. You cannot find your own way out of your Illusion. There is no place in this world and this life you can call Home and you are most certainly yet to Remember all that you have Forgotten to Forget.

The Divine has made sure there is absolute abundance for you in all ways, Always. But it can only ensure this is so when you choose it all of the time.

In choosing the Divine, you will experience abundantly, in time, Health, Wealth and Happiness. It is, however, hard to fill a glass that is already full. Where you have already filled your own glass to the brim, the content is muddied from the Ego, the Divine will need to Clean Up and rearrange.

You may experience "The Glass of Finances" for example, being emptied before being replenished many times more, Likewise Relationships, Health, Surroundings, and many many things the Ego currently values. You may experience Fear whilst a Divinely Chosen Glass is being emptied... of course Fear can only come from the Ego... so instead ask, Why is the Ego so afraid that it would give me this Fear.

It is Never what Your Mind says it is... it is only Ever Your Mind.

As the Observer You Want to Contemplate... Why is the Ego so afraid? Why is the Ego making this Judgement? Why is the Ego so Angry? Why is the Ego Clinging on to this Illusionary Item (money, health crisis, status etc.)? Why is the Ego in this state of Health Crisis? Why is the Ego Blaming Everyone and Everything for my Experiences? And so on.

Do not Dwell... Do not analyse, Only Contemplate... the asking of the Question is enough, as the Power is in the Noticing at which point a Choice with your Willingness can be made to Look at the situation your mind has created. Look at your mind with the Divine's assistance.

Realise that All of your Problems have already been solved by the Divine.

This is true because your idea of Separation has already been solved by the Divine. You may accept that you are not Separate but that is not your Experience, you still believe you are separate from everyone and Everything. Your experience of Blaming others for your Experiences, Judgement, and everything mentioned above is still a regular Experience in your mind from placing your Willingness with the Ego before and during the point of Experience. It must follow that, if you experienced these things, you have chosen the Ego and Separation.

There is no order of Difficulty in the Divine Solving the Problems you face. Indeed, it has already solved all of the problems you face as well as the World's. With your Willingness, if you really want your Problems solved, you must accept that the Divine knows better, and so will solve your problems in its own way, in its own time. Demanding what you experience as a problem that needs solving immediately is futile and can only be the choice for Ego thinking it knows better... Thus, handing over all of your Relationships and all of your Thoughts to the Divine to do with as it Wishes and sees Fit.

Those with rare illnesses who have been introduced to the Divine through the Teacher have experienced absolute Miracles when they connect Truly and Holy. Imagine Muscles so weakened by extreme Juvenile Dermatomyositis for 20 years, and being one of only seven in the World at this level, they cannot even get off the floor or even hold a bottle of tomato sauce. Imagine Pseudo-seizures so extreme, life is just one seizure after another, lasting 45 minutes a time, six to eight times per day and one of only six in the World. Imagine Endometriosis so debilitating, as a teenager an operation rarely ever prescribed for teens was seen as the only solution until introduced to the Divine. Imagine Ankylosing Spondylitis so crippling the spine is cemented in place with arthritis at the age of 19 and taking more than two hours just to roll painstakingly millimetre by millimetre out of bed each morning. Imagine Ulcerative Colitis at the levels of being Anemic and faced with the constant threat of blood transfusions or removal of one's entire Bowl seen as the only solution until meeting the Divine.

The following imaginings are actual life events from students prior to meeting the Divine, and then their complete transition of experience after being introduced to the Divine by the teacher.

Imagine... living with these debilitating diseases and more... for years and years... meeting the Divine and then within 2 weeks, 1 week, and even 45 minutes after that meeting, being completely free of these diseases with Doctors confirming the same but unable to explain.

Imagine an 8 Figure Turnover Businesses about to shut their Doors, 40-50 staff about to lose their jobs, and with a "chance" meeting from following the Divine's Guidance to be at a particular place at a 4am, then suddenly, instantly having more Business than all of the staff can handle.

Imagine an Entrepreneurs Dream of owning an 8-Figure Building, but the Business is being run into the ground, cashflow-strapped, stressed, and losing sleep. Then meeting the Divine and within two years fulfilling those exact dreams, all paid with cash and a Business so abundant, international Stock Market Companies purchase the Business and Rent the Entire Building for the next 18 years, funding the Entrepreneurs' retirement.

Imagine starting your own Business out of your garage, receiving a totally random call out of the blue in your first month. From that call, fulfilling a twenty-million dollar order, paid 100% in advance to your Business Bank Account before ordering all within the same month.

But of Course... the most important of all...

Imagine... a Happiness so profound, your excitement for life just cannot be contained, a Peace so deep, you can never be shaken, Relationships so supportive and strong, it can only be the work of the Divine itself.

You see, the Divine knows what everyone in the World is thinking and doing all of the time. This is because there are no private thoughts. The Divine also knows what everyone has ever thought and will think and the outcomes of those thoughts.

The Ego, however, is only aware of its own thoughts limited to an individual as its Belief System is based on Separation... the "I"... the "Self".

Ironically, it is even this Separated Belief System of the Ego that is Shared amongst all in this World, at its core however ultimately a sharing of Illusion and nothing.

And so, the Divine will give you the perfect thoughts at the perfect time, motivate you in the perfect way to take action as it shares and motivates thoughts with others miraculously in unison for the Benefit of all.

The Divine welcomes all, never shunning anyone, it is only an individual's choosing and misplaced Willingness that would allow themselves to receive anything less than the ultimate offerings only capable of being bestowed by the Divine.

In the end, it is your Willingness to be woven into the masterful tapestry of the Divine for your Ultimate Experience and Full Expression of yourself.

The Divine is there with you always, you are never alone, have never been alone and will never be alone. You are in Great company for you are always in the company of Greatness.

As well as your Willingness you have time. And there is no Greater Time to meet the Divine fully than Right Now. If for some reason you cannot meet the Divine right now, that is totally ok, there is another 'Now' coming right up.

Whatever area of life your problems arise from... Health, Money, Relationships, Time, Surroundings, Loss, State of Mind, etc. ... Your problems have already been solved. It's only a matter of. "When would you like all of them solved?"... Remembering of course, that you will not know how best to solve all of your own problems, otherwise they would have all been solved already. This is because... what you believe to be the problem is not the problem, it is the symptom.

You have been great at solving some of your own symptoms and notoriously bad at solving others with many yet to resolve. This will go on forever until you choose the Divine because there are Trillions of effects but only One Cause. You are aware of the effects, but not the cause, and you believe that each effect requires a different solution. This is the way you attempt to solve all of your symptoms, one after the other, Trillions upon Trillions of times. How futile is this attempt when all symptoms can be solved by solving the One Cause – **The Belief In Separation** and its Symptoms of Dis-ease, Judgement, Blame, Justification, Anger, Guilt, Shame that attract everything in your life you experience as Problems.

When you allow with your Willingness, the One Cause to be solved for you, all of the symptoms you experience as problems simply melt away, revealing everything that has always been and preserved for you all along.

The Divine is Ready.

Would you like to change Your Mind?. . .

*Concepts from: ***A Course In Miracles***

CATHERINE TÉTREAULT-AYOTTE

THE ERA OF FAITH AND LOVE

My life changed when I became the leader of my ship. Because I chose.

Collaborating with Spirit is all about learning to receive the crossings as blessings. Just like a woman in labor learns to surrender to contractions to open up to the life force that is pushing through her, life creation requires us to open up to what is offered to us, to harness and honor this power of creation that we have when we choose to create intentionally and consciously. I'm here to share with you about the gifts and wonders of collaboration with Spirit.

As a child, I was always competing to be as good as my older sisters, which set up a pattern for my young adult life. That feeling of not being enough, not trusting myself, that made me strive to the point of exhaustion.

Competition was reinforced during my entire academic path. Looking back, I realize how intense it was, that pressure to always be the best. I studied in a private, elitist school. Then I majored in business in a high-performance program. Competition was real fuel. My drive and excellence brought me at a young age into roles with a high level of responsibilities with little or no guidance/mentoring at all. I became an HR Director, sitting on boards of directors and reporting directly to CEOs.

My first real life crisis took place when I was hired in one of the top cosmetics multinational companies. I can see now how much we can create our realities through our intentions. I intended to work in a prestigious company. I called in for that. The company's culture was that of competition. Competition was deeply ingrained, along with hierarchy. **My big boss once told me during my yearly review that "*I was too nice. I needed to be more vicious*."** I did not understand that this was the feedback that I received from the head of HR. I wanted to fit in. I gave my heart and soul everyday to perform, to fill the expectations. However, I thought to myself, *"How could I possibly change the essence of who I am*?"

This triggered my first leap of faith. I chose to leave because my job was misaligned with my values. I needed authenticity in my life. This was the beginning of a long vision quest for a sense of meaning, depth and connection.

It went on. I was job hopping for years, seeking for real human connection, the warmth of the soul. That quality of presence was non-existent and taboo in the corporate system. I kept on manifesting from a place of lack of trust. I could only receive what my limited mind was ready to receive.

After manifesting my last corporate job, HR manager for an organic company, the cycle of mistrust finally broke.

I felt separated from myself there too. I had no space to feel, to exist. My soul was calling me. *You should not be here.* That's when I opened up to divine will.

I cried every morning on my way to work as I listened to the song *Follow the Sun* by Xavier Rudd, to feel the feelings.

Looking back, I can see now that I had the choice to leave all along. I sabotaged myself because I didn't trust Spirit. Instead, I reinforced my victim story. My life changed when I chose not to be a victim anymore. When I took responsibility for my life.

The best part of that story is when I truly realized my capacity to create my life with Spirit's support. On New Year's eve, my prayer was clear and simple: **To create space.** I asked, *"Dear God, please help me create space in my life."*

I had asked for the job over and over again. This time, I left it open. Spirit was able to send me what I really needed. I transmuted mistrust into trust.

Two weeks later, my boss emailed me to request a meeting with me. It came out of the blue. I was on maternity leave. But I knew it right away. And I was right on. **I lost my job and I knew I had manifested it.**

A feeling of relief and joy lived in my heart. I also felt the pain of rejection, but I knew it was life opening up for me. Trusting the invisible was seeded inside of me at that very moment.

I surrendered.

I deeply trusted that I was guided. That allowed the Universe to work it's magic.

IF YOU TRUSTED LIFE, WHAT WOULD YOU CREATE?

I had learned to separate my inner self from my outer self. For protection. Out of separation is created a scarcity mindset, which leads to competition.

The scarcity mindset really has been deeply rooted in our society. Modern Western is based on the following premises: *There will not be enough. If you have it—I won't be able to have it too. The faster the better.*

Modern consumerism and hyper-industrialization have taught us a lifestyle of consuming goods, food, substances and material things, at the center of our lives. **Altars, forests and churches have turned into malls, mansions, A/C and concrete everywhere. Having and doing is more important than being.** We have glorified the masculine principles of getting things done and undervalued the feminine principles such as care, organic rhythm and connection to the earth.

Our humanity is soulless, hungry for deep connection, a sense of meaning and a deep longing for real love. Beauty, nature, poetry, silences, this is what nourishes the soul. Our humanity is longing to find the way back to reconnect to the source of life. The source of beingness. Our humanity lacks initiations. Guides. Meaningful passages. We don't know how to be otherwise, in the non-ordinary reality, in connection to source, to nature. We have forgotten how to talk to the stars and listen to the trees. We have forgotten how to allow for life to unfold. Just like nature knows how to grow flowers and tomatoes. Without forcing. or pushing. But we have forgotten about our elders and their wisdom. We have long forgotten about our mission to sustain life for the 7 generations to come. We have forgotten who we truly are.

MY PERSONAL TRANSFORMATION FROM COMPETITION INTO COLLABORATION

As Spirit supported me to create space in my life, I received the blessing of what I believe is the true community. Sisterhood. Brotherhood.

I will never forget the first day I sat in a circle. That deep feeling of safety. Of being enough. Being seen. Just. As. I. Am. I allowed my wisdom to carry my voice. I received a deep kind of love, the type that fills you up, a connection to an infinite source of love. Inside of me. I was relieved. I thought to myself, "*I finally made it. I belong here.*"

In the circle, I learned to trust again. I received my first initiation into mystery in a caring community, hungry for soul and connection. We sat in duos. We were asked: "*Look in each other's eyes, and tell the story of the little girl that you see in your opposite*". I cried, because I felt seen, in the depth of myself. All those years of working so hard for attention, approval, recognition. All I really wanted was that level of presence and care. I felt witnessed, honored. A deep embrace offered by life. An oasis for a kind of humanity that was forgotten, for connection to something bigger than myself.

As I opened up to Circlework, Soulwork, and the medicine of rites of passages, I discovered the true meaning of reunion - as opposed to separation. **I realized that this was my soul work. Facilitating these kinds of circles.** Holding space for transformation. Connecting to the invisible to support transformational work. And a Mission was created.

From the moment I chose to say yes to the calling of my soul, everything shifted. I manifested allies, tools, mentors, teachers. I followed my soul and it knew exactly where to take me.

I was trained and initiated into being a space holder, harnessing the power of connection to the invisible to create healing and transformation through rituals, rites of passages and ceremonies. When we create a ritual for an individual or a community, we tap into the necessity for them. What is required is a clear intention, an appropriate container and a symbolic gesture. The magical ingredient is to invoke divine guidance. When you call in a force that is bigger than you, you acknowledge that you don't control and you actually accept to be transformed by the mystery. You don't know what is going to happen, you don't know how, but you believe strongly in your intention, you hold that intention, you carry it in you, you infuse it in the space. You also track with the collective, you are fully present to what is unfolding so that what is ready to be transmuted will shift. At the end of a ritual, when you celebrate, you know there was true healing, true transformation.

In parallel to the soul and ritual work, I joined a leadership circle for years, that's where I connected with my true purpose. I received a vision from Spirit: "*Create the spaces that you crave so deeply—infused with trust, safety and beingness. Others need it too.*" I aligned my life with my vision, over and over. I was committed to my path through this circle. I was trained and initiated for 2 years to hold those spaces myself. I received the blessings of my teacher to move forward and offer this medicine.

Spirit orchestrated one of the most powerful life initiations. I started walking my path on the Red Road as I joined the Moondance Community. It represents a way of life, a life choice to live in harmony with nature and all our relations, to embrace a spiritual way of life, to honor the teachings of the elders and to consciously weave the new humanity that we are praying for deeply in our hearts and souls. This work has been life-changing. I learned to dig deeper in courage, humility, and strength to renew my faith. I was building the resiliency that was needed to birth my purpose in the world. I was ready to create spaces of transformation and healing for my community of women.

I faced my resistances, relentlessly. Despite the fears, I opened my first women's leadership circle and it created major transformations for all the women involved, including myself.

I now embody the medicines that were given to me. I received them as blessings from Spirit.

Activating my courage to choose to align my life to my calling and to weave divine connection in my daily reality has required me to **trust** So deeply, with devotion and faith into the invisible.

COLLABORATING WITH THE INVISIBLE / SPIRIT

One precious practice that I use on a daily basis is Connection to Source which was passed on by Lev Natan, a faithful ally and mentor on the path.

- Go to a place in nature, it can be a park if you live in the city. I go to a woodland that is 5 minutes walking distance from my house.
- You enter a ceremonial space within, where you choose to be intentional.
- As you enter nature, you pass a threshold, it could be trees, or whatever calls you. You salute the Spirit of the forest, or God, or the Universe, or Divine mother, whatever resonates with you.
- You speak out loud (you can whisper, as long as your lips move). You name yourself and you ask for guidance. You ask to be heard, to be received. I usually open up with gratitude, because it is an anchor. It teaches me sufficiency. It brings me back to seeing all that is already here. And it sends a clear message to Spirit, "keep sending me that!" Gratitude opens my heart.
- Then, you share what you need. If you need a new pair of shoes, you share that too. You could ask for guidance on a decision that you must take, you can ask for support on a challenging situation that you are facing, you can ask to be shown how to leave a toxic job or relationship. You can ask to be shown a new way to be or how to let go of old ways of competition and struggle.
- Ask to be shown how to align your life to your highest self.
- Share with your heart, with no attachment or expectations. Share wholeheartedly, from a place of integrity with what is alive for you. Share from a place of trust that you won't have to carry all this load anymore. You have entrusted your deep desires to a Source that is far greater than you.
- When you are done sharing, you say THANK YOU. and you go back through the threshold.
- You will feel relieved, you will feel supported. You might receive answers to your questions right away. With such clarity. What you hear here, is your inner wisdom, your inner knowing. It comes from a place that is invisible. You

can't see it but you KNOW. You can trust that. **This is how you start creating an intimate relationship with the invisible thread of life that guides you.**

When you connect to Source on a daily basis, you learn to trust as life unfolds in front of you with ease and flow.

I teach deeper practices of connection to divine guidance in my transformational programs and I also work with experiencial practices such as rites of passage and Earth medicine ceremonies to experience deep spiritual connection, empowerment and manifestation/life creation.

DELEGATING THE 'HOW' TO THE DIVINE / GREAT MYSTERY

What does it mean to collaborate with Spirit and co-create your life with divine guidance?

First of all, it means that **you surrender to a force greater than you.** You agree to bow your head in front of the mystery and the wisdom of the heart. You choose to stop fighting. You accept that Spirit will come into your life to support you and inspire you. Inspiration. In Spirit.

Second of all, it means that **you accept that you don't know HOW it's going to happen, but you know it will.** You are responsible for a clear vision for your life: The what and the why. What do you long for so deeply? It starts with a feeling. Go deeper to feel the root of that feeling. It is essential. Just like water is essential for life to carry on. It is an art to feel the feelings, to bring forth what is inside, outside, to find the right words to translate your vision into the tangible and then to orchestrate aligned actions and courageous changes to get on this thread of guidance for your life, which is yours to reclaim.

Third of all, it requires **you to activate your will, your volition**, which is the driving force that pulls you forward. It means that you get to take actions that *will* make you feel uncomfortable. Showing up in new ways can be destabilizing and can bring up insecurities. There are practices to secure your nervous system. I teach those self-healing practices, rituals and ceremonies to support women in their transformational journeys.

And finally, what is required is that **you say YES to the CALLING**, knowing that it will come with a crossing, **where you will choose to let go of the old and embrace the new.** The cycle is simple: 1) You say yes to the calling. 2) You ground deep to feel the resistance and then go through the crossing. 3) You choose the new conscious way. 4) You receive the BLESSINGS!

At last when you harvest, you receive yourself. You receive the abundant flow of life that is life giving and infinite possibilities. It is trust. It's so soft, real and healing. You realize it was worth it to trust, to jump in the mystery of life. Then you REJOICE! You feel connected, supported, you literally see and feel Spirit everywhere. In the sun rays, the bird that comes and visits you, in the songs you hear. You feel connected to the interconnectedness. To the web of life and relations. To Oneness. **And that is the most healing and nourishing experience one can live.** Feeling like you are part of a tribe, you belong on this earth, you are one with the elements, you feel the softness of the Earth holding you, that life force, the Source!

What I've discovered on my journey is that essential step towards collaboration with Spirit: to create space to listen, to soften, **to be receptive,** which is a feminine principle. In the old paradigm, we were taught that getting things done is the most important thing, we have overly glorified the doing. The truth is, we have forgotten how to just BE. The path is about remembering who you truly are and how you can access your power of creation from within. It will require that you choose to believe in the unseen, not the ordinary or usual, and to soften into faith.

IS YOUR FAITH STRONGER THAN YOUR FEAR?

A wise teacher, Dominique Owen, once asked me this powerful question: What do you nourish and feed? Know that your mentality/ego will pull you back into the old ways of overdoing, overcontrolling, burnout, addiction, over-consuming, comparing, and pushing. It's normal. It's a defense mechanism against change. This is how we were all conditioned. Now choosing to show up in integrity, choosing collaboration with self and spirit, will require strengthening your anchor and ground.

This path is about taking full responsibility about who you are, what you manifest and what you stand for in this world. Your vision becomes your compass. Everything that is manifested outside is directly related to what is inside of you.

In the circles and programs that I offer, women experience true sisterhood, where they each learn to take responsibility for their own needs and ownership of their triggers. Integrity is our main anchor and we learn to let go of the old paradigm/wounds of competition, feminine betrayal, victimhood and comparison. We move into sufficiency, then gratitude, confidence, inner power, leadership and impact. In the spaces that I offer, women connect to their power to create the new paradigm and they actively birth their creations in the world.

This new reality is woven in collaboration. The work is so intense and needed, it's literally not possible to do it alone. It is a work of reunion. Reuniting all the parts of you.

May you open your heart to seeing the infinite possibilities of this one precious life. May you deepen your connection with your essence. May you dare to trust. May you love fiercely. May you support one another. May our souls meet and co-create this new era in faith and love.

As I close this chapter, another one opens up: I have surrendered fully to Spirit's guidance. Spirit said: "*let go of all that you hold on to and go back to the Source*". We are packing our bags, out to the jungle, to create a new way of living, in a conscious community in Costa Rica. Follow me to get the full story as it unfolds, in God's timeline.

With all my love and gratitude,
Catherine Tetreault-Ayotte

ABOUT THE AUTHOR

CATHERINE TÉTREAULT-AYOTTE

Catherine Tétreault-Ayotte helps women embody courage to become the powerful creator of their lives. She is a transformational mentor for women who want to go deep within in order to be who they truly are. Starting with the roots, we remove layer by layer to uncover her essence, her vision, and her true purpose. Master manifestor and certified ritualist, Catherine has helped hundreds of women experience transformation, discover their divine essence and spiritual gifts, love themselves, and embrace deep, spiritual connection. She is the Creator of **Women Who Rise Up**, a movement to inspire, guide and empower women to create the New Paradigm.

Catherine is the creator of the **Bold and Embodied Mentorship Program**, a 6-month portal into your truest, most embodied self for women to courageously love themselves, create from their roots, and embrace their fears to create what's calling them deeply.

Catherine created **The Sacred Path of The Priestess Retreats** for women to truly embody their sacred leadership as pioneers of the New Sacred Feminine Leadership Paradigm. During those retreats, we offer interactive experiential journeys to activate, awaken & align our paths to Divine Will. It is a space of true collaboration among leaders as well as a co-creation with Spirit, guiding us to channel in our offerings based on what is required for the collective.

Catherine is also the co-creator of **Florestral Illuminative Project**, an of-the-grid spiritual community based in the Diamente Valley in luscious Costa Rica, where we share a vision of living ceremoniously in harmony and connection with the land and the 4 elements, in a community of growth, love and conscious creation of the New Paradigm.

From this land, Catherine opens portals towards inner essence and she shares the powerful work of initiating women into their sacred medicine and divine essence.

Get a taste of Catherine's medicine here with this free gift:
Unleash your sacred path activation:
https://www.thesacredpathofthepriestess.com/freeactivation/
Join Catherine's community **Women Who Rise Up** on Facebook:
https://bit.ly/3gTmjpd
Connect with Catherine on Instagram:
catherineayotte_themystic
Email: catherine@emergencehumaine.com

KATERINA LENARCIC

GET UP AND KEEP GOING ON YOUR JOURNEY TO EMBODY YOUR HIGHER SELF

The story of my awakening starts at 14 years old. A school friend came over to my house with a little red book which you all know as the Bible. She felt she needed to convert me to Christianity. That evening, I was lying in bed trying to fall asleep, which was difficult because I am empathic and felt the energies around me. I started reading a couple of pages. You must understand religion was not a big factor in my life. Being labeled as a non-Christian or Christian was never important to me. As I fell asleep, I had this vision: I was standing in front of heaven's gates. I had this heavenly feeling about how I was calm and peaceful, a welcoming feeling of love, a knowing that everything was going to be ok. As I was watching the gates slowly open, suddenly out of nowhere my vision changed. In the next scene, I was in a blanket of darkness, a feeling of being cold and not wanted, a feeling of being very frightened about what I saw. And what did I see? Well I saw the devil, my version of what that was at 14 years old. At that moment, I woke up screaming. I just knew I was the light, and why would I be plunged into the darkness like that, what did I do wrong and how could I pull myself out of here? The answer was, "I have agreed to experience the darkness of this physical world. Unbeknownst to me at 14, I would be spending my life transmuting it into the light. As I was crying in confusion, my mother came to me, held me, and just said it was a silly dream and not to take much notice of it. Well, I could not do anything else but take notice. My collaboration with my spiritual self at this time was to journey in the energies of darkness.

So, this was the beginning of my journey, I just knew in my heart I woke up from the illusion of this world and to the fact that there is something much more to me than what I knew and was told to me, by my parents, my schooling and everything I read and heard. This started my dark night of the soul journey, and I walked straight into my higher self 29 years later at 55 years old. At 14 years old I didn't have any self-esteem, I didn't have any value of who I was, and I was always reminded how unworthy I was by the one person that said he loved me: my father.

At 16 years old I was aware of how empathic I was to those around me and the energies around me. I would be given glimpses of the invisible world to just let me know how real it is. I remember one night as I was lying in bed feeling afraid, as I curled up within myself, I suddenly heard a voice of a beautiful, gentle lady who was sitting in a rocking chair in a ghostly way next to my bed and was watching over me. I just knew not to be afraid of her and that she was of the light, unbeknownst to me she was an aspect of my higher self, she calmed me down and she asked me, "What is it that you want?" I naturally breathed into my instincts and my answer was, 1. "To always have a job that will give me the money to be independent", 2. "To be loved for who I am," 3. "To work with Spirit," because I knew then that my purpose in this life was to help as many people as I could through their darkness and to activate their light, to be connected to the higher aspect of themselves that was just waiting to help. The idea of knowing what that would look like and how I would do that just did not enter my thoughts, I was determined as I was laying there to fulfill this purpose.

We all want to know how we are connected to the invisible world, even if we do not have the ideas or structure in doing this. It is part of our human DNA to remember who we truly are, this is our birthright and the gift we gave ourselves. Collaborations with our spiritual guidance will assist us all in manifesting what seems to have been lost when we came into this world. But let me tell you, we planned this to happen because we knew that this journey would bring us back to our mastery of light. My reasons for participating in my evolutionary journey to reclaim my sovereign self and be the example of courage and strength. My purpose is to help my clients understand who their higher self is, to reconnect them to their shadow self, and show them how to connect directly with safety and joy. Yes, even with our shadow we can find joy and treasures that will help us to embody our true natures. It is the toxic shadow we are unraveling and releasing from our energetic space. We all have the capability and self-worth to connect with our higher selves, who are just waiting for us to say, "Yes I am ready", even if you have no idea how. I am here to help you let go of the conditioning of lack of and fear and the disconnection to our light.

My passion within my heart as a 16-year-old was to move out of this fear and into my light of understanding. What did that mean and how was I going to do that? I had no idea, and I was naïve about my journey in my physical form, but I had this determination deep within me that I was going to achieve this invisible connection no matter what my life was to bring me. My journey takes me through the "caves" of my darkness where I learned to face the shadow. I was afraid, but I've learned this shadow was simply ME.

When I ventured out of my cave in 2001, I had a vision of me suddenly waking up in my cave and seeing a river and walls of gold. I felt so much joy and peace. I also discovered a beautiful, strong expansion of light that can only be self-witnessed through my own human eyes, a connection that carries me forward every day with strength, courage, and determination. It has brought to me a light that is so wondrous and healing, and it has brought to me galactic and angelic beings of light that help me to become Katerina, a being of extraordinary light.

Humanity is now being asked by the energetics of the universe, of different places and cultures to tap into their highest selves so they can all have direct communication with their universal counterparts. This collaboration has been in the planning since 2006 when it was agreed by the royal ancient lineage that it is time for the human consciousness to be connecting and learning about who they truly are. Many high-dimensional beings have spent hours adjusting their energies and realigning themselves to their human counterparts to be able to assist in bringing humanity into the next stage of planetary evolution. This must be done, or planet Earth has the timeline to plunge into the darkness for another 250,000 years. This is why the galactic dark royal families are using all they have right now (2021) to create so much fear.

So, this brings me to the conversation of how one individual can connect and have a beautiful relationship with their higher self. Planet Earth is at a pinnacle stage of transmuting this toxic darkness off the planet. The galactic and angelic empires, with those who have passed over, are now coming closer to humanity. It is now time to start introducing them to every human soul on this planet. I have been in communication with Archangel Gabriel since 2019, this started our energetic braiding and now he communicates through my throat chakra and uses my eyes to address you directly. The following section is spoken to you directly from him.

WHY IS IT IMPORTANT NOW THAT WE CONNECT WITH OUR HIGHER SELVES AND OUR GALACTIC UNIVERSAL COMMUNITIES?

"To understand yourselves as being bigger and brighter than you know. To understand that you can create a peaceful world that does not involve the darkness that you had plunged into 250 000 years ago (the fall of Atlantis). You see, to help humanity from total disaster and plunging into the darkest of dark, high dimensional light beings of an ancient lineage are now waking up their human counterparts to assist in the planetary ascension and what you call the Event. These ancient souls have the authority to awaken those human selves that can hold these greater energies that will destroy and remove the dark forces that are upon this planet. And to stop the dark forces from siphoning human energy, this is called loosh. This is why it is important to do your inner work so you can remove these hooks from yourself. Planet Earth is not allowed to be interfered with by other beings from the galaxy. You have free will, but it is humanity that can create the highest frequency to move into your higher selves.

Why is it important that you all understand that being small or having the lack of self-understanding was deliberately created by the Cabal / the toxic shadow to keep you from activating the God spark within your DNA, this has been the target all along? Understand you are part of a major event to have you all look within yourselves to know that each of you has the universe that can be truly felt, seen, and used to your advantage. Your ability to create and manifest is what they want to remove because once you discover this, you have the tools to transmute and remove the Cabal of the planet, and your energies will be clean and aligned and they will not be able to hook themselves into your energetic space. Your higher selves can connect with Mother Earth to communicate the information and light codes that each of you has. This is truly a miracle because it is the human DNA that God placed his energies into. Each of you connects and embodies all the information that will create an Earth of love, abundance, wisdom, and experience. The 3rd dimension is being reconstructed and altered into a dimension where each soul that wishes to go into the higher dimensions must travel through the dark night of the soul because of the individual's history, past lives, decisions, and actions you have created. Why is it important now because these grids and doors of 3D have been closing and disconnecting since September 2019. If you don't make the decisions to evolve then you/your soul will have to take another 1600 years to return to this same point you are in now (2021). The energetics will slow down in this 3rd Dimensional space. Many of you are moving into the 4th dimension as this is written. A huge awakening is occurring.

You are all moving into a timeline where you will have the opportunities to meet your galactic families, but you must be able to look at yourselves in the mirror and truly love who you are. So now is the time for souls to wake up the God spark and this will take you into your darkness because you must unravel all that you have done to cause limitations and fear upon yourselves. You must understand to be able to stand Infront of a galactic or angelic being and not have an emotional breakdown, you must love yourself unconditionally for they have an unwavering sense of self-worth and truly understand themselves completely. When you look into these eyes, your human self will be challenged and this unwavering knowing of who they are will act as a catalyst and break down parts of you that you have neglected. This means it is now time for humanity to face yourselves and clean up your house/soul. Therefore, it is important to clean your energies and realign with your higher self, to do this you must understand your darkness. Yes, you all have been influenced. Your free will is what you need to take responsibility for, only you can ignite and activate the light within you. Your inner work, you're pushing through your challenges, and being proud of who you are is why this ascension needs to occur. Your planet Earth, this beautiful being of light, only wants to see you, her occupants, to flourish, to grow, to bring in more light to the surface. Why is it important NOW? Because you all have the light within you to expand, to create, and manifest such wonderful, successful outcomes on this planet and with your universal counterparts.

There have been many others in your past who have had this connection and they were your forerunners who worked through the hardest density on this planet, and they were able to create a path of more light. Why is it important now? Because the process has quickened, and you can activate your own ascension just as your masters before you. Katerina is one of these forerunners. She can help the collective and help many activate their God spark so they can become their own masters of light. Why now? Because the Universe, your brothers, and sisters are counting on you. Be grateful you are here because you will be known in your history books as those who help eliminate and clear the dark forces off planet Earth."

OUT OF THE DARK AND INTO THE LIGHT

My collaboration with spirit has been a journey of wonderful discoveries about how our Universe, our spiritual guidance are assisting us. Looking at my journey I have discovered with such profound amazement that it has always been about how I was taught to maneuver within my own darkness, how to see all that is about me without fear and how to not judge myself. At another pinnacle moment of my journey, I had a car accident in 1988, I found myself standing in front of a "cave" with a celestial being, Archangel Gabriel. I asked why I was here and he said, "You need to go into this cave". I was afraid and certainly not aware of the bigger picture. I asked why and he said, "You need to go into your own darkness to learn how to walk and see in the dark without the light so you can switch on your golden, grandest light, then you will be able to rid the world of its demons. When you know how to switch your light on, with your courage and a strong sense of self, then nothing can stop you from being the human being of much sovereignty and wisdom. This gift will be yours to share with others to show them how to master their own light by mastering their own darkness. Be assured I will always be with you and when you return into your light a beautiful world of abundance and higher frequencies await you."

Intuitively, I said yes, which started my path to my ascension. In 1992 I was introduced to Navaro, my celestial galactic being of light, who helped me start my new life. During my journey I find myself moving into a new place and relationships in the year 2000, under the instructions of my guidance. While driving to my mentor's home in

2007, he said hello telepathically and told me he was back in my life to be my personal teacher and mentor between 2007 to 2016. He introduced me to Zachariah (angelic) and Tah'el, my galactic connection. During my spiritual self-isolation, I was taught how to sit with each of them, connect and consciously communicate with all of my senses, and most important to learn how to trust myself. They taught me how to identify different energies, who they were, where they were located in the universe, and what was their purpose. This is how I developed my Blue Diamond Team. He taught me how to give myself consent so they could assist me in my journey. Higher-dimensional beings have been coming into my life and are assisting me in understanding what energy is, how that works through the human body of our emotional, mental bodies. He showed me how to work with my shadow and this is how I found my strength to go deeper within myself to retrieve my ancient light that I hid from myself and the Universe so I wouldn't get hurt during the galactic wars.

I have successfully created deep, meaningful relationships with my Blue Diamond Team who assist me in building my self-worth, self-value, and self-empowerment, and now I help others to retrieve and activate that within themselves. My collaboration has taught me how to transform and acknowledge my understanding of who I am as a human being and how my unique light can serve humanity.

I sit for hours and communicate with my celestial beings who light my path so I can love who I am, feel worthy of my gifts, and most importantly feel proud of being a celestial being having a human experience. They are always wanting me to understand how worthy I am of my awakening.

You see, your journey is about finding yourself and knowing unconditionally that you have the power to move great depths of density to make room for your grandest light. We cry and laugh together as we take this journey, no matter how long it takes. They help me to gain my understanding to be the best human being I can be and not allow the dramas of this world to distract me from my mission.

Archangel Gabriel always says to me, "Get Up and keep going on your journey to be your highest version, even when it feels like you are not able to. This always means that you are just about to uplevel into the higher version of yourself and this is how I help you."

Be Your True Self, is my business I created on 10 August 2016. I create a safe space for my clients to journey into the depths of their hearts to retrieve their treasures. I connect them to their higher self that wishes to be acknowledged so they can have a wonderful relationship, to tap into all the tools and solutions they need to embody in this life. I give my clients my tools like Crystal Light Bed Healing and Light Language activations and Reiki and my personal connections to my Blue Diamond team. I help them to develop an understanding of self-worth and how to keep their energies clean from any negative influences.

Thank you for reading my chapter. I am very grateful to have had the opportunity to share it with you. With love and support, and wishing you all the 'aww' and 'aha' moments that will bring you joy, just as it has for me. I am now in my grandest light to show and teach many how that can be YOU.

I will leave you with a message from Blue Diamond Team and Archangel Gabriel: "Everything at the right moment, my dearest friend; you will see how beautiful and bright you are. Every connection you make helps you to become your unwavering self-worth and this is your gift to humanity. Know that everything you require is available for you, you just simply need to say YES to your Evolutionary Growth of Self".

Special Offer

If you resonated with my Chapter, I would love to offer you a special 30 min Higher Self Reconnection Session. Bookings: https://beyourtrueself.setmore.com. Code: Gabriel.

ABOUT THE AUTHOR

KATERINA LENARCIC

Katerina Lenarcic is a Quantum Light Master and Activator working with Universal Life Energy.

It is not until you must look closely at who you are, that you will find the light within your darkness, a journey to become your higher self.

Katerina has developed her own understanding of her humanity and her universal self. With her wisdom, experience and understanding she will walk with you to remember how you are your own Master of life.

Katerina works with her clients to give them a safe place to re-discover their connections with their higher selves and spiritual guidance. They are taken on a journey into their own interdimensional energy field where they are guided by Archangel Gabriel, her oversoul and the angelic world, and with her Blue Diamond Team of higher dimensional beings of the galactic universe, such as Nehkmet of Sirius Lyran Council, who have so much love and support to give you on your journey of self, and they work with her healing tools of light language and Crystal Light Bed healing and Reiki.

Her clients establish a profound relationship with their higher selves which brings them clarity, helping them to understand how worthy they are of manifesting their dreams. Her clients always leave her feeling lighter, brighter, with an "aha" moment, knowing they are able to move forward with ease and grace.

Links
Website: www.beyourtrueselfkaterina.com
Booking calendar: beyourtrueself.setmore.com
Email: beyourtrueself111@gmail.com
Facebook business page: www.facebook.com/katerinalenarcic
Light Language private group:
https://www.facebook.com/groups/lightbluelanguage/
Special Price book offer: 30 min conversation to reconnect with your Higher Self. $97 AUD valued at $155 (code: Gabriel)

OLIVIA JOY GRACE

CO-CREATION WITH SPIRIT: THE DANCE OF EXISTENCE

DESIRE: THE SOURCE OF EXPANSION

As a young child I knew I had a great purpose and gift to give to the world. I told my mother I was an angel sent down to help others be happy. Throughout my life, I held on to that mission and did anything I could to bring more joy to those around me. Many times I accomplished this at the expense of my own joy, which got the least of my attention. I felt trapped in the throes of depression and anxiety and from my lower perspective, lasting happiness seemed out of my reach. A defining moment for me was at my first job in The Mall of Georgia. I watched herds of people walk by day in and day out and noticed how unhappy most of them appeared to be. Not many of them were smiling or playing, but had grimaces and frowns upon their faces as they entered and left the mall. I noticed it did not matter their age, color, gender, or whether they were with a partner or child, or if they were all alone. The dissatisfied look on their faces connected them all, despite the other differences in their appearances. During my observation, I saw that although the majority seemed defeated and down, there was a small percentage that seemed happy and lively. This small group also had no distinct color, age, or gender that connected them all. This observation sparked a deeper interest in happiness inside of me. I wondered what common things these people had that the others were missing. I longed to be a part of the happy group and had an immense curiosity to uncover how to make this a reality for myself and others.

Soon after this desire to be happy planted itself in my brain, I began doing research to uncover the secret to happiness. One night, in the midst of an intense anxiety attack, I decided enough was enough. I feared my head would surely explode if the thoughts in my mind did not settle down. I googled "how to be happy" and information on Buddhism came up in the results. I dove into the world of mindfulness and meditation and felt an immediate resonance with the information provided. Spirituality felt right to me and I craved more understanding. Next, I searched "best books about spirituality" and the book ***The Secret*** by Rhonda Byrne was at the top of the list. I thought, 'what a funny coincidence that I am searching for the secret to happiness and I've found a book called "The Secret"'. I read the book and it confirmed what I had always suspected: there is much more to life than what we see at first glance.

The synchronicity had a snowball effect as I began attracting all sorts of information about meditation, mindfulness, and manifestation. My best friend also had a spiritual awakening around the same time as me and was sharing her findings with me. I sat outside one day and received a text from her asking me, "Did you know your thoughts are creating your reality?" Just reading the text sent chills over my body. It rang true to a deeper knowing that I was slowly but surely becoming aware of. I felt a sense of peace wash over me and thought to myself, "This moment could only be better if he were here." "He" was a guy I was dating at the time. Immediately a text came through from the exact person I was thinking of. It was an unmistakable confirmation from the Universe that what my dearest friend had shared with me was true. From that moment on I became obsessed with understanding how our thoughts form into reality and how I could use this finding to create lasting joy in my life.

ONENESS: SEEING LIFE THROUGH THE EYES OF SOURCE

One of the great lessons I learned early on in my spiritual journey is the truth of oneness. I came to understand that we are not only one with our fellow humans, but with our planet, our animals, our Universe, and the divine energy that creates worlds. Competition stems from fear, and fear stems from the illusion of separation. When living and acting from fear, there is always something to defend, protect, assert, or prove. There's a notion that there is a "them" over there and an "us" over here. This leads to the idea that in order to prosper we must belittle, discredit, and even harm the competition so that everyone knows who has won, and who is right. Many people often feel a disconnect from their own inherent self-worth. They seek to revitalize their self-esteem by being superior to others. Not knowing that they are ever-expanding beings, and no accomplishment will ever be enough, they get trapped in the cycle of chasing accolades and recognition, like a horse chasing a carrot on a stick. What they don't know is that their worthiness is God-given and always has and always will belong to them.

When you know you are worthy already, there is no need to measure yourself up against another. When you recognize another as an extension of not just you, but the divine loving energy present in everyone, you automatically reach a level of respect and compassion that embraces the perceived differences, rather than using them to prove right vs wrong or superiority vs inferiority.

Our existence is like a stew made of and by Spirit. We are the various ingredients that make up the rich, delectable soup. Imagine a carrot competing with a celery demanding that the celery recognize him as the superior vegetable in the soup and the celery feeling less than and questioning his part in the dish. If we know anything about a good stew it's that every vegetable, seasoning, and spice brings its own unique flavor to the dish. No one ingredient is better than the other. It is the wonderful collaboration and coming together of every single ingredient that creates a great meal.

Becoming aware of my collaboration with Spirit brought my existence from mediocrity to eternal, evolving wonder. Before I knew my true Essence, my desires scared me because I doubted my worthiness and ability to actualize them. Now every aspiration inspires and excites me. I know it is a knock at my soul's door from the Divine, signaling that there is something new it wants to experience through me. Before I knew my infinite nature, problems would stress me out and leave me feeling defeated and weak. Now, every problem is an opportunity to remember who I am and expand beyond my previous, perceived limitations. Before I understood my oneness and connection to everything and everyone, my interactions with others illuminated my insecurities and fueled my poor self-image. Now, every rendezvous with a person is an example of how love, synchronicity, and reflection abounds in this plane.

INADEQUACY: THE ILLUSION NECESSARY FOR GOD TO BECOME MAN

Do you ever feel like you don't measure up to the expectations that your or others have of you? Do you ever feel like your daily endeavors and goals are driven by the need to uphold these expectations? Do you ever feel inferior or inadequate when comparing who you are, what you have, and what you've achieved against who others are, what they have, and what they've achieved? Realizing your inescapable collaboration with Spirit eliminates any feelings of low self esteem, or a general "not-enoughness". It also completely eradicates the need for any sort of comparison. The Universe is infinitely expansive and omnipotent, meaning it is present in each and every person/thing. Source Energy is what we all are at the core of our being, so who are we really comparing ourselves to? On a fundamental level we can only really be measuring ourselves up against innumerable versions of ourselves. We are all God manifested as something appearing to be lesser and separate. Even if we did have something to compare ourselves to, what could be greater than God?

When I became aware of these truths, I understood there is no reason to compete because we have all already won. I am in my own lane, in my own reality, creating! Knowing I am much greater than my manifested human "self" crumbles the walls of restriction and settling for less. It opened my mind to what Deepak Chopra calls "infinite potentiality". This concept allows me to know that anything I can conceive of is not only possible, but available to me in a parallel reality that I can select. It doesn't matter what you've been choosing or what you previously thought. All that matters is what you choose to select now, in this moment.

Creating reality from the skillset and perspective of a mere human is taxing and time-consuming. Your efforts are constantly thwarted by the tug of war between proving your worthiness and doubting your worthiness. Each state of mind gives way to the other and perpetuates the cycle of self-sabotage. KNOWING (not hoping, wishing, or wanting) but knowing the infinite and all of its power dwells within you allows you to manifest your desires with much more ease and pleasure. There's no pressure in making it happen by a certain time because you know that everything is unfolding perfectly. There's no need for it to hurry and become physical so that you and others can experience it with your physical senses. The exhilaration you feel from accepting your desires as yours is fulfilling enough. There's no strain to take unnecessary, needy action because you trust the Universe to deliver all that you've chosen.

AWAKENING: WE CAME TO FORGET JUST SO WE COULD REMEMBER

Though we are all collaborating with Source at all times, obviously we are not always doing so in a way that brings us joy. I've come to know that this is not by accident and that our troubles, shortcomings, and low points in life lead us to our greatest expansions.

We came here to feel all up and down the emotional scale and to remember that we have a choice. We can choose how we feel regardless of what goes on around us. By choosing how we feel, we also directly and consciously affect the world around us, and inside of us. This is the basis of conscious creation and collaboration with Source. First you see what is, you observe what has been created. Second you accept what is instead of pushing against it. Thirdly, you make a choice to either continue giving that circumstance your attention, emotions, and energy; or to give attention, emotions and energy to the preferred circumstance. When we find ourselves in lower vibrations, those moods usually spring from deep-rooted fear. Our all knowing God-self knows there is nothing to fear and that everything has already worked itself out. A question you can ask yourself before you react in any moment is, "is this response coming from love or fear?" Many times our poor choices or hurtful actions come from us attempting to protect our wounded inner child from further harm. When we remember who we are, we know we don't need to protect him/her, but to let him/her know there is nothing to fear and that all is well. Some of you may read this and think, "But all is not well!" and since you know your thoughts and feelings are creating reality, that statement reflects exactly why that is so. When you remain certain that all is well, your reality must reflect that to you. When you let go of that fear your joy and vibration rises. Raising your vibration allows you to vibrate with Source energy and create like a God.

Learning that I had the power to create anything I wanted changed my entire outlook on life. I was 90% certain that my life would be impossibly mediocre if not devastatingly unhappy before I understood manifestation. I then felt like I knew how to help others become happy. I began telling everyone I knew about how they could create their reality. I quickly learned that not everyone is interested in that kind of power. Many people associate taking responsibility with taking blame and they are too comfortable being a victim. Being a victim to life and creating reality are opposite ideals. Because we are undeniably powerful, we can identify as a victim and therefore create a life in which we are victimized. This is why owning all of your creations is imperative to mastering manifestation. I read a quote by Abraham Hicks that read, "Tell everyone you know: 'My happiness depends on me, so you're off the hook. And then demonstrate it. Be happy no matter what they're doing. Practice feeling good, no matter what.'" In that moment, I realized nothing and no one has control over me and my emotions until I grant them that privilege. I understood that by labeling others as the cause of my problem, I also dubbed them as the one responsible for my solution. This meant I would have to wait around for everyone who had ever offended me to come to their senses and change, to please me. Knowing I couldn't wait for that day, I stopped blaming others for the problems in my life and began creating. I saw that my power wasn't in controlling and governing others, but in controlling and governing myself. My power lies in my reactions and responses to what happens to me. I now ask myself, "What meaning am I assigning to myself based on this interaction? Is that true? Does that meaning I created serve me?"

DECIDE: NOW THAT I KNOW I CAN HAVE ANYTHING, WHAT WILL I CHOOSE?

I craved freedom from the rat race of the "regular world" and wanted to express myself authentically. Many people have a similar desire, but are held back by the fear of leaving the job that offers them security. My fear of a mundane existence and desire to be liberated outweighed my fear of uncertainty and possible failure. I dove into the unknown and left my job as a waitress and started my coaching business, "Master Manifesters", in which I help women consciously create their desires into their lives. My clients take an inward journey and rediscover their true Self and power while pursuing their current desire. It seems to them that the prize comes when their goal is realized. The real reward is learning how to create not just this one thing but the next and the next. The gift is not just what you get but who you become in the process. Mastering manifestation causes you to become more loving to yourself and others, more grateful for what you do have, more trusting in the Universe and overall, more like God. In my coaching program we focus on six main points that allow creation to be done consistently and without excessive effort.

HOW I HELP OTHERS

The first thing we explore is three main Universal laws that directly affect your ability to create what you want into your life. The Law of Attraction, put simply, states that your thoughts, beliefs and feelings are attracting the circumstances and people in your life experience. The Law of Vibration suggests that circumstances and people that are in consistent close proximity are vibrating at a similar frequency. The Law of Assumption dictates that we are the causation of everything in our lives and that our reality is only what we are assuming it to be.

Once we know the basics, we get specific. All and any realities are available to you now, which one would you like to experience? What people? What things? What emotions? At this point during coaching, many clients realize they've never given serious thought to exactly what they want because they never felt it mattered, let alone that it could actually be possible.

Next we focus on eliminating doubt. Doubting your dreams and yourself is a sure way to destroy your desires before they are even given a chance to manifest. Constantly questioning yourself and your power takes the fun and ease out of manifesting. When you accept that you can, in fact, have anything you choose, the world opens up to you. You no longer accept less than you deserve because you know you have the option to create something that resonates with you.

While coaching with me, we also identify and release blocks, resistance, and limiting beliefs. When you have a desire and a belief that opposes that desire, you have a block. This is the reason not every single thought we have manifests. We can only create what is mostly aligned with our beliefs. Many of our blocks are hidden in our subconscious and we are unaware of why we can't seem to manifest this specific thing. The way to uncover a block is to look objectively at your reality, what is the story it tells about you around that circumstance?

As I mentioned previously, consciously manifesting as a human requires a lot of work. Endless scripting, constant asking, and second guessing yourself the whole way towards what you want. In my Master Manifester Coaching Academy we focus on occupying a state of not just someone who has their desire, but someone who is aware of their power and ability to create whatever they choose.

Lastly we focus on raising and maintaining a high vibration. The more we expand and remember who we truly are, the higher our desires vibrate. This perpetuates the cycle of wanting more and becoming more, which manifests as the infinite expansion of the Universe. As individuals, we experience that expansion physically when we create lives more full than we ever dreamed possible and inspire others to do the same.

Collaborating with Spirit is inevitable because Spirit is present in all. Being aware of your collaboration with Spirit gives you the opportunity to steer your life exactly where you want it to go. Alan Watts described life as a ballroom dance. The point is not to get from one side of the floor to the other. The point is in the coming together, the flow, the expression, the dance. The point is in the collaboration with Spirit, of two embodying the energy of one.

Experience is a much better teacher than words. I invite you to enjoy a free 30-minute session with me where I will reveal your blocks, and help point you in the direction of your desire.

ABOUT THE AUTHOR

OLIVIA JOY GRACE

Olivia Joy Grace, also known as "The Manifestation Queen", is a transformational Law of Attraction Coach. She assists women in identifying limiting beliefs and blocks in their self concept. This allows her clients to break through their perceived glass ceiling and experience the next level in their life, partnership, and/or business.

Olivia guides her clients to their highest vision by shifting their paradigm and therefore creating a new reality that is much more aligned with their ideal, unlimited self.

Her clients receive the necessary tools to transmute not only their current obstacles but any and every inevitable hurdle they may come across during their lifelong journey.

Olivia uses her extensive knowledge of universal laws along with an abundance of love and compassion to wire in the infinite, limitless version of the awakened woman.

You can connect with Olivia here:
Facebook Group:
https://www.facebook.com/groups/995504270887613/
Youtube:
https://www.youtube.com/channel/UCCP48bJi856F4khOSXp13ow
Instagram: @master_manifesters
Website: https://manifesters.wixsite.com/life

ABOUT HILLE HOUSE PUBLISHING

Hille House
PUBLISHING

Krystal Hille founded Hille House Publishing in early 2021 in answer to the call of collaborating with thought leaders so that collectively, we can bring human consciousness to a tipping point to embrace personal power and sovereignty.

Krystal Hille is a Soul Leadership Coach, Embodiment Teacher and Founder of Hille House Publishing. She is passionate to gather conscious entrepreneurs who align with her mission to awaken and empower humanity into deeper levels of sovereignty and connection. She helps her clients share their stories and expertise in multi-author bestselling books to enhance their authority and create more impact in the world.

With 30 years in leadership, a background in theatre directing and female empowerment, Krystal is a multiple international #1 bestselling author, winner of the CREA Brainz Global Business Award 2021 and host of the Soul Leadership Podcast.

Aware of her multidimensional self, pre-Covid, Krystal facilitated spiritual retreats to Egypt and ran the Temple Nights across Australia.

She holds a BA in English Literature & Theatre Studies, a diploma in Life Coaching and TimeLine Therapy and is a certified Tantra Teacher and Reiki Master. She is a popular contributor to international festivals, summits and podcasts and has written two solo books and contributed to a further four anthologies.

Originally from Germany, Krystal lives with her two children in county Victoria, Australia.

If you would like to join future multi-author books or write your solo book through Hille House Publishing, connect with Krystal here:

Website: https://krystalhille.com
Email: krystal@krystalhille.com
Facebook: https://www.facebook.com/krystal.hille
Youtube: https://www.youtube.com/c/KrystalHille

Printed in Great Britain
by Amazon